marshmallows

100 MOUTHWATERING MARSHMALLOW TREATS

TIM KINNAIRD

marshmallows

100 MOUTHWATERING MARSHMALLOW TREATS

APPLE

A Quintet Book

First published in the UK in 2014 by
Apple Press
74-77 White Lion Street
London N1 9PF
United Kingdom

www.apple-press.com

ISBN: 978-1-84543-520-2
QTT.MMLL

This book was conceived, designed, and produced by
Quintet Publishing Limited
4th Floor, Sheridan House
114-116 Western Road
Hove BN3 1DD
United Kingdom

Project Editor: Julie Brooke
Designer: Lucy Parissi
Photographer: Jon Whitaker
Food Stylist: Uyen Luu
Art Director: Michael Charles
Managing Editor: Emma Bastow
Publisher: Mark Searle

Manufactured in China by 1010 Printing International Ltd.

10 9 8 7 6 5 4 3 2 1

CONTENTS

INTRODUCTION

Food has the ability to do many things. It can excite, soothe, tease or comfort. Some food is serious, other food is light and passing. Marshmallows … well marshmallows are the mischievous children, staying up late laughing, smiling and telling jokes until you can't help but join in their bouncy party.

The recipes and advice in this book are intended to be relaxed, easy and – more than anything else – fun. Happily, most people don't know how easy marshmallows are to make. The basic recipe is something that, with practise, can be made in 10 minutes with only four ingredients. Hooray for that. Wowing your co-workers with some – they were just something I made at home – triple layered marshmallows, couldn't be easier. Walk tall at the school cake fair as your home-made salt caramel marshmallows sell out first. Throw out those self-help books – marshmallows are the key to social success and personal contentment. Honestly.

Marshmallows originate from the mallow plant. *Althaea officinalis* is native to Europe and Africa and, when crushed, releases a thick, gloopy mucilage. In ancient Greece it was recommended to relieve wounds, swellings and all sorts of inflamed body parts. Apparently, it was particularly efficacious once boiled in wine. The ancient Egyptians first used it as a food and to set a confectionery made from egg white and sugar. As with much of today's sweets, the French refined the marshmallow in the nineteenth century and started using gelatine in place of the plant extract.

Most commercially available marshmallows are far removed from those early original treats. What's widely available now has its place, but is dense and dull compared with what you will quickly master at home. Using egg white as the basis of marshmallows is the key difference and gives them a light and delicate texture.

We make and sell lots of marshmallows in our shop. On quieter days or, if we're feeling virtuous, we give out free marshmallows to try. The response is always the same: 'oh, that's lovely – it's so light'. More than anything else we might try, it surprises.

Then there's what happens to marshmallows when you heat them up. Melting marshmallows under a flame transforms them from fun sweets into a complex mix of burnt sugar and molten vanilla. With marshmallows, still waters run deep. From the simple s'more to marshmallow-infused cocktails, melt them and they turn edgy.

Making marshmallows is an excellent way to experiment and get creative in the kitchen. While a light and fluffy vanilla marshmallow is perfect in itself, it is also a springboard for a journey into a sweet and bouncy universe. Let marshmallows be your confectionery canvas. Marshmallows are easily flavoured and do a remarkable job of losing their intrinsic mallowyness and absorbing the flavours around them. That's what the recipes in this book aim to achieve.

As important as clear and bright flavours are, marshmallows work because of their texture. Their bounciness requires chewing and that heightens the flavour. Contrasting that with crunchy, creamy or even fizzy coatings adds immeasurably to the eating fun. It increases the surprise and excitement.

Shaping and moulding marshmallows is easy. Modern silicone moulds and baking tins offer an infinite world of shaping. From geometric shapes, bûches, twists and lollipops, master the basic recipe and there are hours of fun to be had. Another side to marshmallows is their property as a ready-made recipe component. Think of them as pre-prepared meringue. For adding both texture and flavours to mousses, icings and toppings, they are a brilliant store cupboard emergency item.

However, more important than anything else, marshmallows and their recipes should be light-hearted and relaxed. Channel your inner eight-year-old, make a mess and get sticky!

INGREDIENTS

The simplicity of marshmallow making means you can source the core recipe ingredients easily.

Some ingredients work particularly well in marshmallow making. Really good natural fruit extracts and oils should be your best friend and will make the job of flavouring much easier. A few drops added at the last second will transform a mix before setting. Good quality chocolate and unsweetened cocoa powder will make or break any chocolate creation. A basic marshmallow is a blank canvas for flavour and the chocolate used will shine through.

SUGAR

Sucrose and glucose

Sugar… is sugar, right? Wrong. For successful marshmallow making you'll need sugar in the forms of sucrose and glucose.

Sucrose in the form of caster sugar is the majority of the sugar used in these recipes. Don't be constrained by plain white caster sugar though.

Try unrefined variations and even brown sugar to make your marshmallows. They will add complex caramel and vanilla tones and work as a flavouring in themselves. See the brown sugar marshmallow recipe on page 56.

Glucose adds nothing to the taste of marshmallows, but it is used to stop the sucrose from crystallizing. This is particularly important if the marshmallows are to be stored for a while. Handling and measuring glucose syrup can be the definition of sticky. Wet

Gelatine

Gelatine can be hard work as the strength and preparations vary. All the recipes here are written for platinum strength leaves. Bloomed sheet gelatine is the easiest preparation to incorporate into a whisking marshmallow mix. As a rule, one leaf will set 80 ml (2 ¾ fl oz) of liquid. Most recipes in this book require 5 sheets (8 g/¼ oz) of platinum strength gelatine.

Gelatine is also available as a powder, but converting between the two is complicated because strengths vary, so I recommend using leaves. However, if you want to use powder, look at the package to see how much liquid it will set, then work out how many packages you will need and follow the package instructions.

Some of the recipes in this book will give softer set marshmallows than others. Chocolate and higher fat ingredients will thicken the mix. Fruit purées and any additional liquid will give a lighter but wetter result. The final texture also relates to the amount of gelatine used. Feel free to add another sheet or take one away according to your taste.

Eggs

Use eggs that are a few days old. As eggs are stored, the egg white component becomes more liquefied. This form of egg white whisks up a little more readily and will give your marshmallows an even lighter texture. The same effect can be achieved if you separate your egg whites in advance and store them in a covered bowl overnight in the fridge.

Colourings

Make use of the natural food colourings that are available. The colour will heighten the taste. Colourings can also be used to decorate. Once a marshmallow is poured into a tin to set, swirl dots through it to give an appetising ripple.

your hands and any tools used to measure it out, such as spoons, spatulas etc. A good tip to stop the glucose syrup from sticking to the bowl when transferring it to a saucepan for heating, is to spoon the glucose out onto the weighed-out sugar. The sugar will coat the sticky syrup and make it easy to tip out.

EQUIPMENT

Free-standing mixers

There's a road that most home bakers and confectionery makers travel down – the road to a free-standing mixer.

At first, you use whisks and wooden spoons. An easy step up is the hand-held electric whisk. At the end of that road is the free-standing mixer. Maybe you'll be inspired by a new job, birthday or divorce, but one day you'll have an epiphany and buy one – and you will wonder how you ever got by without it. They make marshmallow making easy. Yes, it is doable without, but it is harder work. Go on ... you deserve it.

Thermometers

You'll need something accurate and digital, and no, that old meat thermometer that tells you when your turkey is done isn't going to cut it. Choose wisely. An instant-read digital sugar thermometer is preferable as the temperature of the sugar syrup rises quite quickly toward the magic 120°C (250°F) and your thermometer needs to keep up. A thermometer that clips to the side of the saucepan and holds the tip nicely in the middle of the syrup frees up your hands. You need to ensure that the thermometer isn't touching the bottom of the saucepan or else you'll get an inaccurately high reading.

Bowl scrapers and spatulas

A bowl scraper and offset spatula are invaluable tools in handling and shaping the warm marshmallow mix. Running the spatula under warm water before smoothing the marshmallow helps flatten and shape it more easily.

Piping bags and moulds

Shaping marshmallows is half the fun of making them. Fill a piping bag with marshmallow mix and you can easily pipe mini marshmallows to tumble into hot chocolate or long strips that can be twisted into shapes. Silicone moulds are great for creating perfectly smooth and even shapes. Lightly oil the moulds and fill with marshmallow mix for a sharp finish.

Storing

Marshmallows benefit from a period of time at room temperature and exposure to the air before storing. This helps them develop a slight crust as they mature and dry out. That gives a great textural contrast. After that, store them in an airtight container and eat within a week to ten days.

Food allergies

Happily, none of the ingredients in a basic marshmallow recipe contain gluten. It's also easy enough to choose variations of that recipe that use gluten-free flavourings and coatings. Also included in this book are recipes for egg-free and vegan marshmallows.

THE VANILLA MARSHMALLOW MOTHERSHIP

The start of your marshmallow journey begins here. This is the core recipe on which many of the variations that follow in the book are based. There's a bit of technique and judgment required in perfecting the lightest and most delicious marshmallows, but not that much.

Using egg white in the recipe gives a much lighter marshmallow. (See pages 12 and 13 for egg-free and vegan recipes.) Basically, this recipe is a meringue made with hot sugar syrup that is combined with gelatine. That's as easy as it sounds.

Making marshmallows can be messy. In many ways that's half the fun of making them. Unless you want to find crusted-on bits of sugary goodness behind your ears two days later at work, prepare and plan. If you're not bothered, dive straight in and immerse yourself in sticky sweetness. Mmm.

INGREDIENTS
For about 30 (2.5-cm/1-in) marshmallow cubes

Plain marshmallow:
5 sheets (8 g/¼ oz) platinum-strength leaf gelatine
1 teaspoon vegetable oil
1 egg white (35 g/1 ¼ oz)
300 g (10 oz) caster sugar
1 ½ tablespoons glucose syrup
1 teaspoon vanilla extract (or other flavouring)

50/50 coating:
50 g (1 ¾ oz) icing sugar
50 g (1 ¾ oz) cornflour

METHOD

1. Place the gelatine sheets in a bowl of cold water and leave them to soften or 'bloom'. This should take about 10 minutes. Make sure the water is cold. If it's warm, the gelatine will start to melt.

2. Lightly grease a 20-cm (8-in) square baking tin with the oil.

3. Place the egg white in the bowl of a free-standing mixer. A hand-held electric mixer can also be used. Mix together the caster sugar, glucose syrup and

4 tablespoons water in a small saucepan until the mixture feels like wet sand. Place a digital sugar thermometer in the saucepan and bring to the boil over medium heat. There is no need to stir the mixture. As you heat the sugar syrup, sugar crystals may form on the side of the saucepan. A heat-proof pastry brush dipped in cold water can be used to dissolve and disperse this sugar. When the syrup reaches 115°C (240°F), start to whisk the egg white until it forms stiff peaks.

4. After 4–5 minutes the sugar syrup will hit 120°C (250°F). Pour it slowly and carefully down the side of the bowl while whisking the egg whites at medium speed. Avoid pouring the hot sugar syrup onto the beaters as they will spray hot sugar around the kitchen and cause lumps in the mix.

5. While the meringue mix is whisking, squeeze the excess water from the gelatine sheets. After 2–3 minutes, add the softened gelatine sheets directly into the mix, still continuing to whisk.

6. Add the vanilla or other flavouring.

7. Continue to whisk for an additional 3–4 minutes until the mixture is thick and stiff. The mix needs to hold its shape but still be workable. You can't overwhisk at this stage, but if it cools too much, the marshmallow will be very difficult to shape or mould. You'll never get it out of the bowl!

8. Scrape the warm mix out into the greased baking tin and smooth evenly with an offset spatula.

9. Mix the icing sugar and cornflour in a small bowl. Dust the top of the marshmallow with a fine layer of the mixture and leave to set for 4–6 hours or preferably overnight. Cut the marshmallow into chunks and drop them into the sugar and cornflour mixture to coat them. Store in an airtight container for up to 1 week.

TIPS

Most marshmallow recipes recommend dusting the bottom of the baking tin with cornflour and icing sugar before you pour in the marshmallow mixture. I think this makes it harder to spread the marshmallow evenly. When dusted, the warm marshmallow mix has a tendency to move around as one lump and pockets of icing sugar and cornflour can form underneath. Greasing the tin allows the marshmallow to be removed easily and produces a smooth, flat bottom.

50/50 MARSHMALLOW COATING

The 50/50 icing sugar and cornflour coating used here is used throughout this book and should be your go-to coating. It can be livened up easily with colourings and flavourings such as fruit powders, finely chopped nuts and edible lustres.

FREE-FROM VARIATIONS

Marshmallows can be made easily without egg. The gelatine alone gives the marshmallow its structure. It's worth trying this recipe, as it gives a slightly denser marshmallow and it's even simpler than the egg white-based version.

EGG-FREE

INGREDIENTS

1 teaspoon vegetable oil
5 sheets (8 g/¼ oz) platinum-
   strength leaf gelatine
300 g (10 oz) caster sugar
1 ½ tablespoons glucose syrup
1 teaspoon vanilla extract
   (or other flavouring)
1 quantity 50/50 coating
   (see page 10)

TIP

All the recipes in this book will work well using this variation. You'll achieve a slightly different result texture-wise, but it will still be delicious and lovely.

METHOD

Lightly grease a baking tin with the oil.

Soak the gelatine sheets in a bowl of cold water until soft. Squeeze out the excess water from the gelatine sheets and place in a small saucepan with 2 tablespoons water.

Meanwhile, heat the caster sugar, glucose syrup and 4 tablespoons water in a small saucepan over moderate heat until it registers 120°C (250°F) on a digital sugar thermometer.

While the sugar syrup is heating, warm the gelatine over very low heat until it melts. Pour the molten gelatine into the bowl of a free-standing mixer and whisk for 2 minutes.

Pour the hot sugar syrup down the side of the bowl onto the gelatine while still whisking. Be careful to avoid the actual beaters or you'll cover the kitchen with hot sugar. Whisk until the mixture is stiff and thick but still workable. Add the vanilla or other flavouring and tip out into the greased baking tin.

Dust the top of the marshmallow with a fine layer of 50/50 coating mix and leave to set for 4–6 hours or preferably overnight. Cut the marshmallow into chunks and coat them in the 50/50 coating mix. Store in an airtight container for up to 1 week.

Makes 20 (3-cm/1 ¼-in) marshmallow cubes

VEGAN

This recipe is fascinating. It's worth trying even if you're not following a vegan diet. The egg white is replaced by a soy protein and the gelatine by a seaweed extract called carrageenan. It's based on the open source recipe from Dave Soleil's blog: www.veganmarshmallows.blogspot.co.uk.

INGREDIENTS

1 teaspoon vegetable oil
5 tablespoons soy protein isolate
(see notes below)
2 teaspoons baking powder
¼ teaspoon guar gum
300 g (10 oz) caster sugar
(see notes below)
1 ½ tablespoons glucose syrup
1 tablespoon carrageenan (see notes below)
1 teaspoon flavouring
1 quantity 50/50 coating
(see page 10)

NOTES

The soy protein isolate can be found in health food shops and the pharmacy section of some supermarkets. Otherwise, it can be obtained online.

Carrageenan is sold as vegegel or vegetarian gelatine in supermarkets. Check the ingredients on the package. It can also be bought online.

Check the vegan credentials of your caster sugar with the manufacturer's website.

METHOD

Lightly grease a baking tin with the oil.

Mix together the soy protein, baking powder, guar gum, and 180 ml (6 fl oz) water in the bowl of a free-standing mixer. Whisk for 8–10 minutes. The initial pale brown paste will be transformed into a lighter white cream and stiff peaks will form.

Next is the tricky part. Place the caster sugar, glucose syrup and 120 ml (4 fl oz) water in a large saucepan and stir to combine. Warm slightly over medium heat until you have a smooth syrup. Sprinkle in the carrageenan and whisk it in to incorporate. Stir continuously, using a digital sugar thermometer to measure the temperature. The carrageenan will naturally cause the sugar mixture to set around the sides of the saucepan. Use a stiff spatula or spoon to keep the sides as clear as possible. Otherwise, the stuck sugar will begin to caramelise, discolouring the mix and creating lumps. Continue to heat to 110°C (230°F). By this stage, the mixture will be thick and extraordinarily sticky. Swiftly tip the syrup onto the soy protein mix while still whisking. Don't scrape in any sugar that has stuck to the sides of the saucepan as it will cause lumps.

Continue to whisk until stiff and thick, then add flavouring, tip out into the greased baking tin and leave to set.

When the marshmallow is set, cut and dust with the 50/50 coating mix.

Makes 30 large marshmallows

FLAVOURING, COATING & SHAPING

Tempting as it is to use the phrase 'let your imagination run wild' to convey the sense that flavouring, coating and shaping your marshmallows should be seen an opportunity to go bananas in the kitchen, I'll resist the temptation, but . . .

In the following recipes there are lots of flavour combinations. Many of those are tried and tested classics, some a little unusual. Any sweet flavour combinations you might come across in cakes, confectionery, chocolate or ice creams will almost certainly work well in a marshmallow.

Incorporating flavours can be a little tricky, as some ingredients will cause the marshmallow mix to collapse and fail. Those ingredients high in fat are particularly difficult. Chocolate causes problems because the cocoa powder butter will flatten your whisking mix within seconds. The best method is to fold the chocolate in at the last minute or coat the marshmallow in chocolate.

FLAVOUR DROPS, OILS & EXTRACTS

An extraordinary range of flavour compounds and drops is available. In supermarkets, vanilla, lemon, coffee, rose and orange water are easy enough to find. Look beyond the baking ingredients section for other inspiration. Dried whole and ground spices such as cardamom, saffron, cinnamon and even pepper make good choices. Finely grind them as part of a coating or infuse into the sugar syrup to flavour the marshmallow itself.

Specialist confectionery and chocolate suppliers stock a wide array of flavourings in the form of extracts and essences. From mandarin to orchids and blue cheese to apple pie, the choice is vast. Natural extracts tend to make better marshmallows and are much more wholesome. See Resources, page 144, for information on where to get hold of them.

FRUIT POWDERS

Freeze-dried fruits in the form of whole fruit and powders are fabulous at packing flavour into a marshmallow. Both can be used as an ingredient in the marshmallow itself, but perhaps it is even better to use a fruit powder as part of the coating.

USING CORDIALS & SYRUPS

Off the shelf fruit cordials are a ready-made marshmallow ingredient. Pour in 3–4 tablespoons during the final marshmallow whisking for both flavour and colour. Look out for the more unusual flavours as well as soda syrups – root beer marshmallow anyone?

OTHER COATINGS

If you can coat a chocolate, cake, biscuit or confectionery in it you can almost certainly coat a marshmallow in it. Chopped nuts and chocolate flakes are great. Ice-cream toppings such as sprinkles work wonderfully. Think about textural contrast.

MOULDING MARSHMALLOWS

Silicone moulds are your friends here. There's a universe of sizes and shapes available. Getting marshmallows out of moulds can be difficult, so go for the less intricate. Geometric shapes work best – your favourite magic unicorn mould is going to be much more tricky.

CUTTING MARSHMALLOWS

For me, marshmallows should be precise and even. In our shop we use a confectionery guitar cutter, which cuts perfect straight marshmallows every time. Unless you're planning on setting up your own marshmallow business, they are a bit expensive. Use a long, sharp knife and try and cut the marshmallows straight down. It's easy to cut them on a slope. Make lots of marshmallows and practise. A greased pizza cutting wheel can work well to get an even cut, as can a cheese board and wire.

PIPING MARSHMALLOWS

A piping bag filled with warm marshmallow is one of the best things to hold. What you do with that bag is almost irrelevant. Think of your piped beauties as confectionery hand warmers and hold them close. If you must make marshmallow with it . . .

Try using fluted tips for small stars or plain tips for domes and mounds. Whatever shape you choose, work quickly. Marshmallow sets fast and it's easy to get distracted and clog up your tip. A piping bag is also a great help for filling shapes and moulds.

Chapter 1

CLASSICS

Soft, sugary and so very moreish, these classic marshmallow flavours
have been pleasing our palates for generations. Whether you enjoy
traditional vanilla or Middle Eastern orange and pistachio, these sweet
treats will delight you and your family for decades to come.

BLACKENED VANILLA SUPER MARSHMALLOWS

So there's vanilla, and then there's real vanilla. Think of vanilla like you would wine – different climates give different flavours. This is your chance to track down some heady, sticky and plump vanilla beans and drift away on a marshmallowy cloud.

INGREDIENTS
4 vanilla beans
1 quantity 50/50 coating (see page 10)
1 quantity ingredients for vanilla marshmallow mix (see page 10)

METHOD
Preheat the oven to 200°C (400°F). Place 2 of the vanilla beans in the oven and bake for 20–25 minutes or until crisp and brittle. Leave to cool, then grind to dust in a spice grinder.

Mix the vanilla dust with the 50/50 coating in a medium bowl.

Split the remaining vanilla beans and scrape out the seeds. Make the marshmallow mix following the method on page 10, adding the seeds to the mix at Step 6.

Leave marshmallow to set, then cut and dust with the vanilla, sugar and cornflour mix.

Makes 30 marshmallows

TOP TIPS
As well as Madagascan, try vanilla from Tahiti, India, Mexico or Uganda (see Resources, page 144). Check out those floral, fruity and chocolaty aromas.

RICH CHOCOLATE-SWIRLED MARSHMALLOWS

Obviously, you need to know how to make chocolate marshmallows – perfect to lift the spirits or eat on the couch while watching TV. Use the best chocolate you can – they will only be as good as the goodness swirled into them. Add the chocolate at the last minute and mix it in quickly.

INGREDIENTS

1 quantity ingredients for vanilla
   marshmallow mix (see page 10)
50 g (1 ¾ oz) plain chocolate
1 quantity 50/50 coating
   (see page 10)
2 tablespoons unsweetened
   cocoa powder

METHOD

Make the marshmallow mix following the method on page 10. While it is having its final whisk, melt the chocolate in a heat-proof bowl set over a saucepan of barely simmering water (bain-marie or double-boiler). Be careful to ensure the water isn't touching the bottom of the bowl.

When the chocolate has melted, remove 3–4 large spoonfuls of the marshmallow mix and mix it together with the melted chocolate until smooth and a deep brown colour. Pour this mixture into the remaining marshmallow mix and quickly swirl it through. You need to just incorporate it – if you do more than that, the mix will become dense and lose its lightness. Spread into a greased baking pan and leave to set.

Mix together the 50/50 coating and cocoa powder in a medium bowl and dust the marshmallows in it.

Makes 30 marshmallows

VARIATIONS

Instead of using melted chocolate, 3 tablespoons of unsweetened cocoa powder can be sieved onto a small portion of the marshmallow mix and then swirled through the remaining mix.

Try coating the chocolate marshmallows in other chocolaty treats. Use chocolate sprinkles or chocolate curls created by scraping a knife over the top of a big bar of chocolate.

Add the seeds of a vanilla bean or a small espresso to the mix just before mixing with the chocolate. Both vanilla and coffee will enhance the rich chocolate flavour.

SPICED CHERRY MARSHMALLOWS

If a marshmallow could be a place and time, these would be curled up in front of a log fire after a long leafy fall walk – boots lined up by the back door with a cat purring on your lap. That is the spiced cherry marshmallow. Eat them.

INGREDIENTS

180 ml (6 fl oz) cherry cordial
2 star anise
1 cinnamon stick
6 cloves
2.5-cm (1-in) piece of fresh ginger (skin on)
1 quantity ingredients for vanilla
    marshmallow mix (see page 10)
60 g (2 oz) dried sour cherries,
    coarsely chopped
1 quantity 50/50 coating (see page 10)

METHOD

Pour the cherry cordial into a small saucepan and add the whole spices. Bring the cordial to the boil, then lower the heat to a simmer for 5 minutes. You want the volume to reduce by about half. Remove the whole spices.

Make the marshmallow mix following the method on page 10. Just after adding the sugar syrup to the egg white, pour the reduced spiced cordial onto the mix. Add the gelatine and continue to whisk until thick and voluminous. Mix in the dried cherries then spread into the greased baking tin.

When set, cut and dust the marshmallows in the usual way with the 50/50 coating.

Makes 30 marshmallows

TOP TIPS

This recipe would work well with other fruit cordial and dried fruit combinations.

Combining the marshmallows with a coating that has a complementary freeze-dried fruit powder mixed through further heightens the fruit tang.

SALTED CARAMEL MARSHMALLOWS

Originating from northern France, the combination of salt and caramel is slowly taking over the world's flavour palate. It works well in a marshmallow because the salt tempers the sweetness. Be brave with the amount of salt and how far you take your caramel. Make 'em dangerous.

INGREDIENTS

For the caramel:
50 g (1 ¾ oz) caster sugar
100 ml (3 ½ fl oz) double cream
25 g (1 oz) butter
½ teaspoon sea salt flakes

1 quantity ingredients for vanilla
    marshmallow mix (see page 10)
Seeds from 2 vanilla beans
1 quantity 50/50 coating
    (see page 10)

METHOD

Make the caramel first. Measure out the sugar, cream and butter. It's important to be prepared and in control when making caramel – hot sugar burns like nothing else and you need to be careful.

Place the sugar in a medium saucepan and heat gently over moderate heat. Move the sugar around the saucepan by gently tipping it. It's okay to stir the caramel when using this method if it's melting unevenly. As soon as it has turned a light brown colour, pour in the cream and butter. This creates lots of steam and fussing in the saucepan. The caramel will seize and look awful, but keep stirring and the sugar will melt back into the cream. Once it has all melted and is smooth, cook over moderate heat for 2 minutes or until thickened slightly. Add the salt and leave to cool.

Make the marshmallow mix following the method on page 10. Add the seeds from the vanilla beans at the end after the final whisking. Pour the liquid caramel into the marshmallow mix and fold in briefly. The process of scraping the marshmallow mixture out of the bowl into the baking tin will combine the caramel and marshmallow, so don't overmix. You want the caramel to swirl and ripple through.

Leave to set overnight, then dust with 50/50 mixture. The caramel makes the marshmallows a little wetter so they will not keep as well.

Makes 30 marshmallows

TOP TIPS

A world of amazing salts are available now, from black volcanic salt to smoked and flavoured salts. Experiment to see which you prefer.

LEMON & LIME SHERBET MARSHMALLOWS

The natural sweetness of the marshmallow is tempered by sharp lemon and lime. What makes these such a refreshing delight is the incorporation of fruit zest and fizzy sherbet coating – absolutely delicious.

INGREDIENTS

1 quantity ingredients for vanilla
    marshmallow mix (see page 10)
Zest of 1 lemon
Zest of 1 lime, plus extra for decorating
Juice of ½ lemon
Juice of ½ lime
50 g (1 ¾ oz) icing sugar
1 teaspoon citric acid
    (see Resources, page 144)
1 teaspoon bicarbonate of soda

METHOD

Make the marshmallow mix following the method on page 10. Incorporate the lemon and lime zest and juice during the final whisking at step 7. The mix will loosen after the juice is added, but whisk it back up to stiff peaks before spreading it into the baking tin to set.

In a small food processor or spice grinder, mix together the icing sugar, citric acid and bicarbonate of soda. This should give a fine dusty powder.

Cut the marshmallows to size then dust and decorate with lime zest just before serving. These marshmallows won't keep well once dusted as they become sticky. They are best stored uncut, then cut and dusted at the last minute just before serving.

TOP TIPS

Use a fine Microplane grater (see Resources, page 144) to zest the fruit and make sure you grate off only the zest, not the pith. This recipe would work as well with orange, grapefruit or other citrus fruits.

The sherbet coating can be adapted to include flavourings. Try adding freeze-dried fruit or powders to heighten the fruity goodness.

ORANGE, PISTACHIO & RAISIN MARSHMALLOWS

This recipe shows just how versatile marshmallows are, providing a blank canvas for these Middle Eastern and North African flavours – best eaten after a long camel ride with a thick, sweet coffee.

INGREDIENTS

2 tablespoons sultanas
3 tablespoons orange juice
1 quantity ingredients for vanilla
    marshmallow mix (see page 10)
1 teaspoon orange flower water
200 g (7 oz) shelled pistachios

METHOD

Soak the sultanas in the orange juice for about 2 hours until soft and plump.

Make the marshmallow mix following the method on page 10. Add the orange flower water during the final whisking. You may need a little more as the strength of different brands varies. Add according to your taste.

Drain the plump sultanas and fold into the marshmallow mix. Spread into a greased baking tin or mould and leave to set.

Finely chop the pistachios in a food processor or spice grinder. Cut and shape the marshmallows and coat them in the ground pistachios.

Makes 30 marshmallows

TOP TIPS

As with all sweet treats and desserts, these marshmallows work as a consequence of the textural contrasts.

Marshmallows are bouncy and soft. Paired with crunchy nuts and moist sultanas, they give your mouth something to think about. That heightens the taste.

Chapter 2

FRUITY

Fresh fruit flavours help to take the edge off the sweetness of a bowl of
marshmallows. Opt for the pure taste of a single fruit – such as apple,
lemon or melon – or try a cocktail of lemon and ginger, lime and
watermelon or raspberry and pineapple – there's something for everyone.

LEMON & GINGER MARSHMALLOW CHEESECAKE

This marshmallow exists in the nether world of in-between cake and confectionery. Pleasure or pain? You decide. That's probably overstating it. It's a cross between a cheesecake and a marshmallow – that's better. The textural contrasts here are as important as the flavours. Lovely.

INGREDIENTS

1 quantity ingredients for vanilla marshmallow mix (see page 10)
Zest of 2 lemons
100 g (3 ½ oz) mascarpone cheese
Few gingersnap biscuits

METHOD

Make the marshmallow mix following the method on page 10. As a final step, add the lemon zest and the mascarpone cheese. The fat content of the cheese will cause the marshmallow mix to collapse a little and create something a bit denser. That's okay. Leave to set.

Break up a few gingersnaps into fine crumbs. Just before serving, cut the marshmallows up and coat them in the crumbs. These are best eaten within a day or two.

Makes about 20 large marshmallows or 8 'cheesecake' slices

TOP TIPS

Obviously, lime or orange zest would work as well, as would other biscuits. Caramelised biscuits are particularly good here.

APPLE CRUMBLE MARSHMALLOWS

Make sure the apples are tangy and the crumble topping is buttery. The marshmallow gods will do the rest. Eat a spoonful, as required, on rainy Sunday afternoons.

INGREDIENTS

For the crumble topping:
75 g (3 oz) butter
75 g (3 oz) ground almonds
75 g (3 oz) plain flour
75 g (3 oz) brown sugar
Pinch of salt
2 sharp apples (Granny Smith, Bramley or Grenadier are good)
½ teaspoon ground cinnamon
1 quantity ingredients for vanilla marshmallow mix (see page 10)

METHOD

Preheat the oven to 180°C (350°F). For the crumble topping, place the butter, ground almonds, flour, brown sugar and salt in a food processor and mix with the blade attachment until well combined and small lumps start to form. Alternatively, blend the butter into the flour with your fingertips, then add the sugar, ground almonds and salt.

Spread the mixture on a baking tray and bake in the oven until golden brown, about 6–8 minutes. Leave to cool and break up any larger lumps with your fingers.

Peel and core the apples and coarsely chop. Place them in a small saucepan with 1 tablespoon water and heat gently until the apple disintegrates. You need a smooth purée, so if necessary, blend in a food processor or with an immersion blender. Add the cinnamon.

Make the marshmallow mix following the method on page 10 and at step 6, add the apple purée.

Pour the marshmallow mix into a greased baking tin and level the surface with an offset spatula. Sprinkle the crumble mix over the top and press it into the surface to create an even crust.

Leave to set overnight, then serve spoonfuls or cut into small ovals or circles to recreate the appearance of an apple crumble.

Makes 30 large marshmallows

FRUIT SALAD SKEWERS

The sixth-form pupils at my high school ran the tuck shop. It sold Fruit Salad and Black Jack sweets, both a penny each. My fondness for these sweets remains fierce.

INGREDIENTS

2 quantities ingredients for vanilla
    marshmallow mix (see page 10)
Pineapple flavouring (see tips below)
100 g (3 ½ oz) raspberry purée
Yellow and pink food colouring (optional)
50 g (1 ¾ oz) raspberry powder
    (optional, see Resources, page 144)
50 g (1 ¾ oz) pineapple powder
    (optional, see Resources, page 144)
2 quantities 50/50 coating
    (optional, see page 10)

30 bamboo skewers, to serve

METHOD

Make 2 batches of plain marshmallow mix following the method on page 10. At step 6, add the pineapple flavouring and yellow food colouring (if using) to one batch and the raspberry purée and pink food colouring (if using) to the second batch.

Leave marshmallow to set, then cut into even and matching cubes. Dust with the matching fruit powder or use the basic 50/50 coating mix. The marshmallows will keep longer if dusted in the cornflour/icing sugar mix, but the fruit powder will heighten the taste.

Spear 2 marshmallows, one of each flavour, on each bamboo skewer and serve.

Makes 30 skewers

TOP TIPS

Some fruits contain an enzyme that breaks down the proteins in gelatine. These include pineapple, papaya, kiwi and, supposedly, melon, so a natural flavouring extract needs to be used instead. However, the recipe for melon marshmallows (see page 35) works well, as the process of puréeing the fruit denatures the enzyme.

The fruit purée in this recipe can be replaced easily with different shop-bought or home-made purées.

BANOFFEE MARSHMALLOWS

Sweet bananas meet sweet caramel, meet sweet marshmallows. Surely the healthy fruit content balances out the less-than-healthy sugars in this case?

INGREDIENTS

For the caramel:
100 ml (3 ½ fl oz) double cream
25 g (1 oz) butter
50 g (1 ¾ oz) caster sugar
½ teaspoon sea salt

1 banana
Squeeze of lemon juice
1 quantity ingredients for vanilla
    marshmallow mix (see page 10)
1 quantity 50/50 coating (see page 10)

METHOD

First make the caramel. Measure out the cream and butter to have them ready. Place the caster sugar in a medium saucepan and warm gently. You'll need to stand over the pan and keep an eye on it the whole time while the sugar caramelises. Gently swirl the saucepan to help the sugar melt evenly. When the sugar has reached an even light brown colour, add the cream and butter. The caramel will solidify, but have faith and keep stirring. The sugar will melt back into the cream and butter. Keep stirring until the caramel is smooth and thickened slightly. This should take 2–3 minutes. Add the salt and leave to cool.

Peel the banana and purée in a food processor. Add a squeeze of lemon juice to stop the purée from oxidizing and turning brown.

Make the marshmallow mix following the method on page 10 and add the banana purée at step 6. Just before tipping the marshmallow mix out into a baking tin to set, add the caramel and swirl carefully through the mix. Leave to set. The caramel and banana in this mix will give a softer marshmallow, so cut and dust with the 50/50 coating carefully. Best eaten within a couple of days.

Makes 30 large marshmallows

LIME MARSHMALLOW & BARBECUED WATERMELON FRUIT KEBABS

Pairing fresh fruit with home-made marshmallows is a joy. The trick here is to cut the marshmallows and cubes of watermelon to the same size. If you haven't tried barbecuing watermelon before, you must – it's a revelation.

INGREDIENTS

1 quantity ingredients for vanilla marshmallow mix (see page 10)
Juice and zest of 2 limes
½ watermelon

METHOD

Make the marshmallow mix following the method on page 10 and add the lime zest and juice at step 6. Leave the marshmallow to set.

Remove the skin from the watermelon and cut the marshmallows and melon into identical-size cubes.

Light up your barbecue or place a ridged grill pan over high heat. Char the melon on all sides.

When the melon is ready, divide the marshmallow and melon cubes among eight skewers. Serve immediately.

Makes 8 kebabs

TIP

Don't barbecue the marshmallows with the melon from the start. The melon takes a while to cook and the marshmallows will have fallen off the barbecue by the time it's ready.

LEMON CURD-STUFFED VANILLA MARSHMALLOWS

This recipe is a good excuse to immerse yourself in the world of cake and chocolate moulds. Flexible silicone moulds are best for this recipe. There's an extraordinary range available now. These work best in small (about 3.75 cm/1 ½ in diameter) demispheres or even mini muffin pans.

INGREDIENTS

For the lemon curd:
4 lemons
12 egg yolks
200 g (7 oz) caster sugar
200 g (7 oz) butter, melted

1 tablespoon vegetable oil
1 quantity 50/50 coating
(see page 10)
1 quantity ingredients for
   vanilla marshmallow mix
   (see page 10)

METHOD

First make the lemon curd. Zest and juice the lemons and place in a small saucepan on moderate heat. Reduce the juice by half and leave to cool in the saucepan. Combine the egg yolks and sugar in a small bowl then add the melted butter. Pour the reduced lemon juice through a small fine sieve (to remove the zest) into the egg, sugar and butter mixture. Pour the mixture into a medium saucepan and warm over gentle heat until it's transformed from thin and glossy to thick and matt. Leave to cool.

Brush your moulds lightly with the vegetable oil and then dust lightly with a little of the 50/50 icing sugar/cornflour mix.

Make the marshmallow mix following the method on page 10. Pipe or carefully spoon half of the marshmallow mix into the bottom of the moulds.

Fill a piping bag with the cooled lemon curd and pipe a small amount into the centre of each marshmallow mould. Fill the rest of each mould with the remaining marshmallow mix and smooth off the top. Dust the tops of the moulds with the 50/50 coating and leave to set.

Makes 30 large marshmallows

TOP TIPS

You could use shop-bought lemon curd here although it's never as good as home-made. The amounts here will give you leftover curd to spread on toast. The same recipe works well with lime or even passion fruit juice.

Decorate the tops of these marshmallows with a sprinkling of lemon sugar: add the zest of 1 lemon to 100 g (3 ½ oz) caster sugar and blend

MARSHMALLOW DAIFUKU(ISH)

Inspired by the Japanese confection daifuku, in which mochi (a sweet, glutinous rice cake) is wrapped around fruit or red bean paste. Here the sweet marshmallow is balanced by the fresh fruity core. Use all bean paste, all fruit or a mixture of both.

INGREDIENTS

Sweet red bean paste (anko) (see tip below) and/or 15–30 pieces fresh fruit (small, firm fruit such as strawberries and grapes work best here)

1 quantity ingredients for vanilla marshmallow mix (see page 10)

1 quantity 50/50 coating, plus extra icing sugar for dusting (see page 10)

METHOD

Dust your hands and work surface with icing sugar and roll 15–30 small (2-cm/¾-in) balls from the anko bean paste. Place them in the fridge to firm up.

Make the marshmallow mix following the method on page 10 but keep the mix relatively loose and runny. You need to be able to coat the fruit or bean paste easily with it. If the mix is stiff, it will be difficult to use as a coating.

Dust a baking tray with the 50/50 coating.

Push a cocktail stick into the bean paste ball or a piece of fruit and delicately dunk into the marshmallow mix. Swirl it around until well coated. Push the fruit- or bean paste-covered ball off the cocktail stick onto the dusted baking tray. Dust the tops of the marshmallow-covered balls of goodness with more sugar/cornflour mix.

These need to be eaten on the day they are made as the water content of the fruit and/or bean paste will soften the marshmallow mix.

Makes 30 marshmallows

TIP

Bean paste can be bought in 450-g (1-lb) packages. It is available online or in Asian supermarkets. It can be made at home from adzuki beans, water and sugar. It's easy enough to make but takes a while.

MELON MARSHMALLOWS

The perfume and scent of the melon comes through really well in this one, but you need a properly ripe melon. Most varieties work well, but not watermelon. Galia or honeydew melons are my favourite. With slices of top-quality ham or preferably prosciutto, these make a great canapé.

INGREDIENTS

1 quantity ingredients for vanilla
   marshmallow mix (see page 10)
Large slice of ripe melon (about 170 g/6 oz)
Few slices of prosciutto or ham (optional)

METHOD

Scoop out the flesh from the melon and discard the skin. Blend the flesh to a purée in a food processor or press the flesh through a fine sieve with the back of a spoon.

Make the marshmallow mix following the method on page 10. Add the melon purée as part of step 6.

Leave to set and cut into generous cubes. Wrap the cubes in small rectangles of prosciutto if desired.

Makes about 30 large marshmallows

ROSE PETAL MARSHMALLOWS

Fragrant, elegant and delightful. These marshmallows are delicately scented with both rose water and crystallised rose petals – perfect after a hard day shopping on the high street.

INGREDIENTS

4 tablespoons crystallised rose petals
1 quantity ingredients for vanilla
   marshmallow mix (see page 10)
About 1 teaspoon rose water
Natural pink food colouring
1 quantity 50/50 coating (see page 10)
Fresh rose petals, for decorating

METHOD

Using a mortar and pestle, crush the rose petals into smaller fragments about 1–3 mm ($\frac{1}{16}$–$\frac{1}{8}$ in) in size.

Make the marshmallow mix following the method on page 10. Add the rose water during the final whisking stage. The potency of rose water differs remarkably – some brands will need only a few drops, some a tablespoon. Go easy and taste after each addition until you've got a flavour you enjoy. Stop whisking and fold in the crushed crystallised rose petals.

Scrape out the marshmallow mix into a lightly greased baking tin. Drip small drops of the food colouring on top of the mix and swirl through with the end of a spoon or cocktail stick. Leave to set, then dust with the 50/50 coating. Cut into cubes.

Serve the marshmallows decorated with fresh rose petals.

Makes 30 large marshmallows

EARL GREY & LEMON MARSHMALLOWS

Infusing tea into marshmallows is a quick and clever way of adding refined and intriguing flavours. The principle behind this recipe would work for any flavour of tea. It also works well for botanical flavours such as hibiscus, jasmine and chamomile.

INGREDIENTS

2 tablespoons loose-leaf Earl Grey tea
1 quantity 50/50 coating (see page 10)
1 quantity ingredients for vanilla
  marshmallow mix (see page 10)
Zest of 1 lemon
Juice of ½ lemon

METHOD

Divide the tea leaves into two and finely grind one portion in a spice grinder. Place in a small bowl and mix with three-quarters of the 50/50 coating. This will be the marshmallow coating.

Place the remaining tablespoon of tea in a cup and pour over 120 ml (4 fl oz) hot water. Infuse for 5 minutes. Strain the liquid through a fine sieve.

Make the marshmallow mix following the method on page 10, but use 4 tablespoons of the strained tea in place of the water that is added to the sugar to make the sugar syrup.

Add the lemon zest and juice during the final whisking stage. Scrape the marshmallow mix into a lightly greased baking tin. Leave to set, then cut and dust with the tea coating.

Makes 30 large marshmallows

Chapter 3

CHOCOLATE

If you're one of those people who always succumbs to a square of
chocolate, imagine how hard it is to say 'no' to a chocolate marshmallow.
Whether the marshmallows are mixed with chocolate before setting,
coated in it or made up of several chocolate layers, resistance is useless.

EGG-FREE CHOCOLATE & HAZELNUT MARSHMALLOWS ON STICKS

Marshmallow mix is easily shaped into fun shapes and sizes. This recipe proves once again that everything tastes better when eaten off a stick. Consider barbecuing, drizzling in hot chocolate sauce or even having bizarre marshmallow-based sword fights. En garde!

INGREDIENTS

1 teaspoon vegetable oil
1 quantity ingredients for egg-free
    marshmallow mix (see page 12)
75 g (3 oz) plain chocolate,
    coarsely chopped
200 g (7 oz) hazelnuts, toasted
    and skinned

Acetate sheets (see method and
    Resources, page 144)
Adhesive tape
12 long lollipop or cake pop sticks
Disposable piping bag

METHOD

Create the moulds by shaping the acetate sheets into cylinders. Cut rectangles of acetate 10 x 14 cm (4 x 5 ½ in). Join the shorter sides with adhesive tape, overlapping them by 1.25 cm (½ in). Lightly grease the cylinders with vegetable oil and place on a greased baking tray.

Melt the chocolate in a heat-proof bowl set over a saucepan of barely simmering water (bain-marie or double-boiler). Be careful to ensure the water isn't touching the bottom of the bowl.

Make the egg-free marshmallow mix and add the melted chocolate after the final mixing stage. Gently stir in the chocolate just enough to combine.

Scrape the marshmallow mix into a piping bag and pipe into the acetate cylinders. Leave to set for about 30 minutes, then push in the lollipop sticks. Make sure the mix is stiff enough to hold the stick vertically. Leave the marshmallows to finish setting in the moulds.

Finely chop the hazelnuts. Peel off the acetate strips from the marshmallows. They should peel away relatively easily, but it may be necessary to use a small knife or spatula to loosen the acetate.

Roll the marshmallows in the chopped hazelnuts and serve.

Makes 12 sticks

EGG-FREE TRIPLE CHOCOLATE LAYERED MARSHMALLOWS

These are as pretty as they are tasty.

INGREDIENTS

1 teaspoon vegetable oil
2 quantities ingredients for egg-free marshmallow mix (see page 12)
60 g (2 oz) white chocolate
60 g (2 oz) milk chocolate
60 g (2 oz) plain chocolate
1 quantity 50/50 coating (see page 10)
1 tablespoon unsweetened cocoa powder

METHOD

Lightly grease a 15-cm (6-in) square cake tin with the oil.

Chop each of the types of chocolate and place in three separate small heat-proof bowls. In turn, place the bowls over a small saucepan of barely simmering water (bain-marie or double-boiler) and leave the chocolate to melt. Remove from the saucepan and keep to one side. If the chocolate starts to set before the marshmallow mix is ready, then place them back on top of the saucepan for about 30 seconds.

Make a double-quantity of egg-free marshmallow mix (see page 12). When whisking up the mix to its final volume, ensure you have everything ready to mix and layer the marshmallow. Adding chocolate directly to the mix will immediately stiffen it up, so you need to work quickly.

Divide the marshmallow mix among three bowls. Add the white chocolate to one of the bowls. Quickly mix the chocolate through with a spatula and then immediately spread the mix into the base of the cake tin. Put the cake tin into the fridge briefly. Add the milk chocolate to the second bowl of the marshmallow mix and spread that on top of the white chocolate layer. Return the tin to the fridge while you prepare the next layer. Add the plain chocolate to the final third of the mix and spread over the top of the milk chocolate layer. Leave to set, then cut. Mix the 50/50 coating with the cocoa powder and then use to dust the marshmallows.

Makes 30–40 large marshmallows

TOP TIPS

This recipe uses the egg-free variation of the marshmallow mix because chocolate causes the classic egg white version to collapse.

A small offset spatula is an invaluable tool to spread even layers in the tin.

BAILEYS MARSHMALLOW CHOCOLATE HAZELNUT CUPS

Ready-made chocolate cups are a wonderful store cupboard standby. Quickly fill with mousse or fruit and – tah-dah – you're a goddess in the kitchen. Filled with boozy and runny Baileys marshmallows, they make a very grown-up canapé or petit four.

INGREDIENTS

½ quantity ingredients for vanilla marshmallow mix (see page 10)
100 ml (3 ½ fl oz) Baileys liqueur
15 chocolate cups (see tips below)
100 g (3 ½ oz) blanched whole hazelnuts

METHOD

Make the marshmallow mix following the method on page 10. After the final whisking, add the Baileys. Whisk until just combined and smooth.

Divide the mix among the ready-made chocolate cups and place in the fridge to set.

Preheat the oven to 180°C (350°F). Spread the whole hazelnuts on a baking tray and toast in the oven for 8–10 minutes or until golden brown. Coarsely chop the nuts and sprinkle on top of the marshmallow. Serve.

Makes 15 cups

TOP TIPS

Making your own chocolate cups isn't hard. All you require is a suitable mould. Something rigid – polycarbonate works best. Then you fill the moulds with melted chocolate.

Moulds for chocolate cups come in many sizes. Something approximately 4–5 cm (1 ½–2 in) in diameter and depth works well. There are lots of designs available (see Resources, page 144), but many are only available in large quantities, so choose wisely.

MINT CHOCOLATE CHIP MARSHMALLOWS

The use of fresh mint as a vibrant green decoration lifts these treats and balances the rich chocolate.

INGREDIENTS

1 quantity ingredients for vanilla marshmallow mix (see page 10)

Peppermint flavouring

Natural green food colouring

100 g (3 ½ oz) plain chocolate chips

Large handful of fresh mint leaves

3 tablespoons caster sugar

1 quantity 50/50 coating (see page 10)

METHOD

Make the marshmallow mix following the method on page 10. At Step 6, add peppermint flavouring to your own preference, tasting after every 4–5 drops. Add drops of food colouring until you have a pale green colour. After the final whisking, stir in the chocolate chips. Spread the marshmallow mix into a greased baking tin and leave to set. Blend the mint leaves and caster sugar together in a food processor until you have bright green mint sugar.

When the marshmallow has set, cut into cubes and dust with 50/50 coating mix.

Just before serving, dampen one side of each marshmallow by pressing it against a damp cloth. Then press the dampened side into the mint sugar to coat and arrange on a plate, mint coating on top.

Makes 30 marshmallows

CHOCOLATE-COATED MARSHMALLOWS

What's better than a marshmallow? A chocolate-coated marshmallow. Coating things in chocolate can be both gourmet food art and guilty snacking pleasure.

INGREDIENTS

225 g (8 oz) dark chocolate

1 quantity vanilla marshmallows (see page 10)

Decorations such as crystallised violets, vanilla sugar or freeze-dried raspberries

METHOD

Melt the dark chocolate in a heat-proof bowl set over a saucepan of barely simmering water (bain-marie or double-boiler), place a marshmallow on a fork, dip in the chocolate, then leave on wax paper until set. Decorate the chocolates to indicate the flavour of the marshmallow: crystallised violets, vanilla sugar, freeze-dried raspberries, etc.

HOT CHOCOLATE WITH INDIAN CHAI SPICED MARSHMALLOWS

Naturally, hot chocolate and marshmallows are best friends, but this recipe maximises that combo. Inspired by Indian chai spiced tea, these marshmallows melt into the chocolate to give up their fragrant and alluring charm.

INGREDIENTS

1 star anise
Seeds from 4 cardamom pods
½ cinnamon stick
4 black peppercorns
2 allspice berries
2 cloves
½ teaspoon ground ginger
1 quantity ingredients for vanilla
   marshmallow mix (see page 10)
1 quantity 50/50 coating (see page 10)

FOR THE HOT CHOCOLATE:

100 g (3 ½ oz) plain chocolate
½ tablespoon cornflour
1 tablespoon milk powder
About 300 ml (10 fl oz) milk

METHOD

Place all the whole spices in a spice grinder and grind until fine. Pass through a fine sieve to ensure there are no larger pieces. Add the ground ginger to the spice mixture.

Make the marshmallow mix following the method on page 10 and add in the ground spices during the final whisking stage.

Scrape the marshmallow mix into a lightly greased baking tin and leave to set.

Cut the marshmallows. As these are going to be melted, they look better cut into interesting shapes with biscuit cutters – stars, moons, circles, etc. Dust the marshmallow shapes with the 50/50 coating mix.

Make the hot chocolate by finely chopping the chocolate, preferably using a food processor. Mix in the cornflour and milk powder.

For a rich espresso-like hot chocolate, warm the chocolate mix gently in a saucepan with the milk. Stir continuously until smooth. For a lighter, thinner drink use more milk.

Drop a few marshmallows into the chocolate and enjoy.

Serves 4

CHOCOLATE, CHILI & LIME MARSHMALLOWS

A great variation for the recipe to the right is to add in lime. The combination of chili and lime is pert and sparky – a marshmallow to take notice of.

Follow the recipe on the right but add in the zest and juice of 1 lime with the melted chocolate and chopped chili.

CHOCOLATE CHIPOTLE CHILI MARSHMALLOWS

The deep smokiness of the chilis works wonderfully with the rich chocolate.

INGREDIENTS

5 dried chipotle chilis
5 sheets (8 g/¼ oz) platinum-
  strength leaf gelatine
300 g (10 oz) caster sugar
1 ½ tablespoons glucose syrup
75 g (3 oz) plain chocolate
½ quantity 50/50 coating
  (see page 10)
1 tablespoon unsweetened
  cocoa powder

METHOD

Soak the chilis in 180 ml (6 fl oz) cold water for at least 30 minutes. They need to have softened and the water needs to infuse with the chili flavour. Remove the chilis but keep the water. Finely chop the chilis.

Soak the gelatine sheets in the chili-infused water until soft. Place the softened gelatine in a small saucepan with 2 tablespoons of the chili water and melt the gelatine over very low heat. Pour the melted gelatine into the bowl of a free-standing mixer and whisk for 2 minutes until frothy.

Mix together the sugar, glucose syrup and 4 tablespoons of the reserved chili water in a small saucepan. Heat gently until it registers 120°C (250°F) on a digital sugar thermometer, then pour onto the gelatine while still whisking.

Melt the chocolate in a heat-proof bowl set over a saucepan of barely simmering water (bain-marie or double-boiler). Be careful to ensure the water isn't touching the bottom of the bowl.

Once the marshmallow mix has reached soft peaks, add the finely chopped chili and then the melted chocolate. Continue whisking the mix until the chocolate is just combined. Scrape the marshmallow mixture out of the bowl into a greased baking tin and leave to set. Mix the 50/50 coating with the cocoa powder. Cut and dust the marshmallows with 50/50 coating mix.

Makes 20 (3-cm/1 ¼-in) marshmallow cubes

TIP

If you're feeling ridiculously brave, ½ teaspoon of chili powder could be added to the 50/50 coating. Alternatively, try adding a few drops of your favourite hot sauce during the final whisking.

COCONUT, PASSION FRUIT & MILK CHOCOLATE MARSHMALLOWS

Bright and zesty passion fruit combines perfectly with milk chocolate and coconut – a tropical cocktail coated in chocolate.

INGREDIENTS

3 passion fruit
1 quantity ingredients for vanilla
   marshmallow mix (see page 10)
100 g (3 ½ oz) desiccated coconut
150 g (5 ½ oz) milk chocolate

METHOD

Juice the passion fruit. Remove the seeds if you prefer, but hidden within the marshmallow, they make a great textural contrast. However, these marshmallows won't store well with the seeds in.

Make the marshmallow mix following the method on page 10 and add the passion fruit juice during the final stage of whisking.

Spread the marshmallow mix into a greased baking tin and leave to set. Cut into cubes and dust with the desiccated coconut.

Melt the chocolate in a heat-proof bowl set over a saucepan of barely simmering water (bain-marie or double-boiler). Be careful to ensure the water isn't touching the bottom of the bowl.

Line a baking tray with wax paper. Dip one side of each marshmallow into the melted chocolate. Let the excess chocolate drip off, then place the marshmallows on the wax paper to set, chocolate side up.

Makes 30 large marshmallows

Chapter 4

EXTRAORDINARY

A twist on the traditional, these marshmallows will delight your
taste buds with their unexpected flavour combinations. From the
timeless pairings of peanut butter and jam, or lavender and honey, to
the Asian-inspired pandan and coconut, or saffron and cardamom,
find something new here.

LAVENDER & HONEY MARSHMALLOWS

These are as fresh and floral as a traditional garden party. Different types of honey
will impart subtly different flavour tones. I favor set honey and freshly picked lavender.
Eat outside with a cup of hot tea.

INGREDIENTS

5 sheets (¼ oz/8 g) platinum-strength
    leaf gelatine
1 egg white (35 g/1 ¼ oz)
300 g (10 oz) honey
1 ½ tablespoons glucose syrup
Lavender extract or fresh lavender flowers
    (angustifolia variety)
1 quantity 50/50 coating (see page 10)

METHOD

Make the marshmallow mix following
the method on page 10, replacing the caster
sugar with the honey and using only
2 tablespoons water for the syrup.

Add the lavender flavouring at step 6.
If using lavender flowers, pick the small
buds carefully from the stems. In both
cases, go easy when adding the lavender;
there is a fine line between delicious and
as overpowering as Grandma's underwear-
drawer liners. You've been warned.

Scrape the mix into a lightly greased baking
tin and leave to set. Cut and dust with the
50/50 coating mix. Decorating with a few
fresh lavender buds would be perfect.

Makes 30 large marshmallows

RASPBERRY, ROSE & LYCHEE MARSHMALLOWS

These are inspired by the Pierre Hermé classic flavour combination in his Ispahan macarons. They are transcendentally beautifully delicious and scrumptious.

INGREDIENTS

100 g (3 ½ oz) raspberries to give
  60 g (2 oz) raspberry purée
150 g (5 ½ oz) lychees to give
  60 g (2 oz) lychee purée
  (see tips below)
1 teaspoon vegetable oil
Natural pink food colouring
½ teaspoon rose water

3 quantities vanilla marshmallow mix
  using the following quantities for
  each batch:
4 sheets (5 g/⅛ oz) platinum-
  strength leaf gelatine
1 small egg white (20 g/¾ oz)
200 g (7 oz) caster sugar
1 tablespoon glucose syrup
3 tablespoons water

2 quantities 50/50 coating
  (see page 10)

METHOD

This recipe involves making and flavouring three batches of marshmallow. Make the purées first. Blend the raspberries in a food processor until smooth. Pass through a fine sieve to remove the seeds. Repeat for the lychees. Oil a 20-cm (8-in) square cake tin with the vegetable oil.

Make the raspberry-flavoured marshmallow, following the method on page 10. Add the purée at the final stage after whisking, then whisk for 3–4 minutes to regain some of the volume. Add a few drops of food colouring. Spread evenly into the greased tin. Put in the fridge to set.

Make up another batch of vanilla marshmallow and add the rose water to flavour together with 2 tablespoons water to thin the mix to a similar consistency to the raspberry layer. Add pink colouring to give a lighter shade than the raspberry. Spread evenly onto the raspberry layer. Return to the fridge to set.

Make the lychee layer in the same way as the raspberry layer. Leave it white. Leave to set. Cut and dust with the 50/50 coating mixture.

Makes 40 large marshmallows

TIPS

For a boozy version, a tablespoon of raspberry liqueur (Chambord), rose liqueur or lychee liqueur (Kwai Feh) can be added to each batch of marshmallow instead of the fruit purées and rose water.

Lychee purée can be found in stores in 900-g (2-lb) quantities. Blending and straining tinned lychees works well or use lychee juice from a carton.

PANDAN & COCONUT MARSHMALLOWS

Pandan leaf is used in Thai and Southeast Asian desserts. It gives these marshmallows a complex, vanilla popcorn-like taste. The coconut dusting adds texture and boosts their nutty flavour.

INGREDIENTS

1 quantity ingredients for vanilla
  marshmallow mix (see page 10)
1 teaspoon pandan extract (see tip below)
Natural green food colouring
100 g (3 ½ oz) desiccated coconut

METHOD

Make the plain marshmallow mix following the method on page 10. After the final whisking, add the pandan extract and a few drops of the green colouring to give a pale green appearance. Scrape the mix into a lightly greased baking tin.

Place the desiccated coconut in a dry frying pan over moderate heat and toast until it turns golden brown and a warm nutty aroma fills the kitchen.

When the marshmallow has set, cut to shape and coat in the toasted coconut.

Makes 30 large marshmallows

TIP

Pandan extract can be bought from Asian supermarkets and stores. It's incredible stuff and can be used to flavour sponge cake, custards and other desserts. Buy some.

BLACKCURRANT & VIOLET MARSHMALLOWS

There is no better sweet flavour combination than sharp zesty blackcurrants and heady floral violets. Decorated with whole crystallised violets, these make an opulent treat.

INGREDIENTS

150 g (5 ½ oz) blackcurrants
1 quantity ingredients for vanilla marshmallow mix
  (see page 10)
Violet flavouring
1 quantity 50/50 coating (see page 10)
Crystallised violets

METHOD

Place the blackcurrants in a food processor and blend until smooth.

Make up the plain marshmallow mix following the method on page 10, adding the blackcurrant purée at step 6. Add a few drops of violet flavouring, tasting as you go until you have the balance you desire. The mixture will have loosened a lot with the addition of the purée, so whisk again for another 4–5 minutes.

Scrape the mix into a lightly greased baking tin.

When the marshmallow has set, cut and dust with plain 50/50 coating. Decorate with crystallised violets.

Makes 30 large marshmallows

BROWN SUGAR & GINGER MARSHMALLOWS

What's brilliant about these is that the natural taste of the brown sugar shines through. The caramel molasses pairs perfectly with the ginger. They make the ideal stocking stuffer.

INGREDIENTS

For the marshmallow:
2 pieces stem ginger in syrup
1 teaspoon vegetable oil
5 sheets (8 g/¼ oz) platinum-strength
    leaf gelatine
1 egg white (35 g/1 ¼ oz)
300 g (10 oz) light brown sugar
1 ½ tablespoons glucose syrup
3 tablespoons water

FOR THE COATING:

1 quantity 50/50 coating (see page 10)
½ teaspoon ground ginger

METHOD

Chop the stem ginger into pieces no bigger than 3–6 mm (⅛–¼ in). Grease a baking tin with the vegetable oil.

Make the marshmallow mix following the method on page 10, replacing the caster sugar with the brown sugar.

Stir through the pieces of stem ginger at the last stage before scraping the marshmallow mix out into the greased baking tin to set.

Combine the 50/50 coating and ground ginger in a small bowl. Once the marshmallow has set, cut and dust with the coating.

Makes 30 large marshmallows

PBJ MARSHMALLOWS

Peanut butter and jam works in any snack: sandwiches, cakes, sweets and definitely in a marshmallow. In this recipe, the peanut butter is used in its purest form – warmed and drizzled.

INGREDIENTS

100 g (3 ½ oz) fresh raspberries
1 quantity ingredients for vanilla marshmallow mix (see page 10)
10 g (¼ oz) freeze-dried raspberries
   (available in supermarkets and online)
½ quantity 50/50 coating (see page 10)
150 g (5 ½ oz) smooth peanut butter

METHOD

Place the raspberries in a food processor and blend until smooth. Pass through a fine sieve to remove the seeds.

Make the marshmallow mix following the method on page 10. Add the raspberry purée to the mix at Step 6. Whisk again for 4–5 minutes until the volume has returned. Add half the freeze-dried raspberries, stir through, then scrape out into a lightly greased baking tin and leave to set.

Blend the remaining freeze-dried raspberries with the 50/50 coating mix. Once the marshmallow has set, cut and dust with the raspberry coating. Warm the peanut butter in a saucepan and drizzle over the marshmallows just before serving.

Makes 30 large marshmallows

TIP

These can be made as a two-layered marshmallow, one layer being the raspberry recipe above and the second layer being a plain mix flavoured with 6 tablespoons peanut butter. However, the peanut butter will make its layer rather dense.

COLA MARSHMALLOWS

This recipe is a good example of utilising what is available in supermarket aisles. Shop-bought cola flavouring paired with a sherbet coating recreates the beverage.

INGREDIENTS

1 quantity ingredients for
   vanilla marshmallow mix
   (see page 10)
50 g (1 ¾ oz) cola flavouring
50 g (1 ¾ oz) icing sugar
1 teaspoon citric acid
   (see Resources, page 144)
1 teaspoon bicarbonate of soda

METHOD

Make the marshmallow mix following the method on page 10. Add the cola flavouring at Step 6, then whisk back to firm peaks and maximum volume. Scrape into a lightly greased baking tin and leave to set.

Place the icing sugar, citric acid and bicarbonate of soda in a food processor and blend until you have a fine sherbet powder. Dust the marshmallows with the sherbet just before serving as the mix will make the marshmallows become damp over time.

Makes 30 large marshmallows

MILK & COOKIES MARSHMALLOWS

It's kind of clever just how much these taste of milk despite there only being a relatively small amount of milk in them. Covered in biscuit crumbs, they are really rather tasty.

INGREDIENTS

1 quantity ingredients for
   vanilla marshmallow mix
   (see page 10)
300 ml (10 fl oz) milk
Few of your favourite biscuits,
   crumbled – Oreos are
   particularly good here

METHOD

Make the marshmallow mix following the method on page 10, but replace the 4 tablespoons water in the sugar syrup with 4 tablespoons milk and soak the gelatine sheets in the remaining milk.

When the milk and sugar syrup is added to the egg white, the mix will collapse. Keep whisking and the softened gelatine will start to cause the volume to rise. Scrape the marshmallow mix into a lightly greased baking tin. While the marshmallow is still warm and tacky, sprinkle with the biscuit crumbs. Leave to set, then cut into pieces.

Makes 30 marshmallows

ESPRESSO MARSHMALLOWS

Elegant and understated. These look best as perfect cubes presented with coffee at the end of a meal with good friends. Good coffee = good marshmallow.

INGREDIENTS

For the marshmallow:
5 sheets (8 g/¼ oz) platinum-strength
　leaf gelatine
150 ml (5 fl oz) cold espresso
　(or strong coffee)
1 egg white (35 g/1 ¼ oz)
300 g (10 oz) caster sugar
1 ½ tablespoons glucose syrup

For the coating:
1 quantity 50/50 coating (see page 10)
1 ½ tablespoons unsweetened
　cocoa powder

METHOD

Make the marshmallow mix following the method on page 10, but soak the gelatine sheets in the espresso instead of water to soften. You'll need to place the gelatine in a shallow dish or bowl so the espresso completely covers it.

At step 6 of the method, add 4 tablespoons of the espresso to the mix. The mix will loosen a little, so you'll need to bring it back up to peak volume with another 4–5 minutes whisking.

Scrape the mix into a lightly greased baking tin and leave to set.

Combine the icing sugar, cornflour and cocoa powder in a small bowl. Once the marshmallow has set, cut and dust with the cocoa powder mixture.

Makes 30 large marshmallows

TIPS

These marshmallows also work well on top of a cup of hot chocolate. Another coffee marshmallow delight can be achieved by putting one vanilla marshmallow in the bottom of a coffee cup and pouring hot coffee over the top.

MOCHA MARSHMALLOWS

An easy variation of the espresso recipe above, is with the addition of 100 g (3 ½ oz) plain chocolate. The joy of this is that the chocolate remains distinct from the marshmallow and forms tiny strata of solid chocolate.

Melt the chocolate in a heat-proof bowl set over a saucepan of barely simmering water (bain-marie or double-boiler). Just before scraping out and setting the espresso marshmallow, add the melted chocolate and fold it in for 2–3 seconds. Don't fully incorporate it – you want a rippled effect.

Scrape out the marshmallow mix and leave to set.

SALTED BUTTERED POPCORN MARSHMALLOWS

It's your favourite movie treat in a marshmallow. This marshmallow works particularly well because of the texture contrast between the crispy popcorn and buttery marshmallow beneath.

INGREDIENTS

50 g (1 ¾ oz) popping corn
150 g (5 ½ oz) butter
½ teaspoon plain table salt
1 tablespoon vegetable oil
1 quantity ingredients for vanilla
   marshmallow mix (see page 10)

METHOD

First, pop your corn. Once the popping gets going, turn the heat off and leave the corn to do its stuff. Melt half the butter. Toss the popcorn in the melted butter with a few pinches of salt and leave to cool.

Line a baking tin with wax or silicone paper, then grease the paper with the vegetable oil.

Make the marshmallow mix following the method on page 10. Add ¼ teaspoon salt into the mix at step 6. Scrape out of the mixing bowl and spread into the prepared baking tin. Leave the marshmallows to cool and set.

Place the cooled butter-covered popcorn in a food processor and blend to small pieces. Melt the remaining butter. Cut up the marshmallow into pieces and coat in the melted butter, then toss in the crushed popcorn.

Makes 30 large marshmallows

GOLD, SAFFRON & CARDAMOM MARSHMALLOWS

Perhaps not an everyday treat, but this recipe illustrates how marshmallows can be elevated to exclusive and cultured delights.

INGREDIENTS

1 tablespoon vegetable oil
6 cardamom pods
Pinch of saffron (see Resources, page 144)
1 quantity ingredients for vanilla marshmallow mix (see page 10)
1 quantity 50/50 coating (see page 10)
Gold leaf – as much as you can afford! (each marshmallow needs approximately 1 sheet)

METHOD

Line a baking tin with wax or silicone paper, then oil the paper with vegetable oil. Crush the cardamom pods and the seeds within them and place in a small saucepan with 3 tablespoons water. Bring just to the boil, then remove from the heat and leave the cardamom to infuse for 30 minutes. Pass the liquid through a fine sieve. Add the saffron strands and leave them to infuse and colour the water.

Make the marshmallow mix following the method on page 10. Add the cardamom- and saffron-infused water at Step 6, then whisk until the mixture forms stiff peaks and reaches maximum volume. Scrape into the prepared baking tin. Leave to set, then cut into cubes.

Dust the cubes with 50/50 mix and place a piece of gold leaf on the top of each one. If the gold leaf doesn't stick easily to the top of the marshmallow, slightly moisten the surface with a drop of water or place the naked marshmallows one side at a time on the gold, completely encasing them in shiny magic.

Makes 30 marshmallows

Chapter 5

GROWN-UP

Who said marshmallows are just for kids? Add a little kick with cocktail ingredients such as rum, gin and Cointreau – or melt marshmallows into vodka for a martini with a hit of sugar as well as alcohol. If you want the sweetness without the intoxication, try the spirit-free variations.

PIÑA COLADA MARSHMALLOWS

Cocktail flavourings work brilliantly in marshmallow form. Alcohol, particularly spirits, is carried well by the architecture of the sugar and egg white.

INGREDIENTS

100 g (3 ½ oz) desiccated coconut
1 quantity ingredients for vanilla marshmallow mix (see page 10)
2 tablespoons light rum
Natural yellow food colouring
50 g (1 ¾ oz) freeze-dried pineapple pieces
   (see Resources, page 144)

METHOD

Place the desiccated coconut in a dry frying pan over moderate heat and toast until a light golden brown colour.

Make the marshmallow mix following the method on page 10. As the final step before setting the mix, add in the rum and a few drops of yellow food colouring. This will loosen the mix, but continue to whisk and the volume will return. This may take 5–10 minutes of whisking until the mixture thickens again as the gelatine sets. Stop whisking and add in the small pieces of freeze-dried pineapple. Scrape out the mix and set in a lightly greased baking tin. When it has set, cut into cubes and toss in the toasted desiccated coconut.

Makes about 20 large marshmallows

TIPS

Fresh pineapple could be used here, but it will make the final marshmallows a little wet and they won't store as well.

ALCOHOL-FREE VERSION

Omitting the rum still gives a tropical, fresh and fruity marshmallow.

THE COSMOPOLITAN MARSHMALLOW

Obviously, you will want to try this one – Saturday night fun without the glass. Go easy. Dropping the alcohol from this recipe still gives a great-flavoured marshmallow.

INGREDIENTS

1 quantity ingredients for vanilla
   marshmallow (see page 10)
Zest of 1 lime
Juice of ½ lime
1 tablespoon Cointreau
2 tablespoons vodka
4 teaspoons cranberry juice
Natural red food colouring
1 quantity 50/50 coating
   (see page 10)
1 orange

METHOD

Make the marshmallow following the method on page 10. At Step 6, add the lime zest and juice. Add the alcohol, cranberry juice and a few drops of the colouring and whisk again. It may take 5–10 minutes until the mixture thickens. Scrape out into a lightly greased baking tin and leave to set. Cut into cubes and dust with 50/50 coating mix. Cut small slices of orange zest and use to decorate the cubes.

Makes about 20 large marshmallows

ALCOHOL-FREE VERSION

Swap the Cointreau for orange cordial and omit the vodka.

SPICED RUM & SULTANA MARSHMALLOWS

Here, plump soaked sultanas are hidden away in pillows of warming spiced rum marshmallow. They're perfect on their own or floating on the top of your favourite hot chocolate.

INGREDIENTS

50 g (1 ¾ oz) sultanas
6 tablespoons dark rum
1 quantity ingredients for
   vanilla marshmallow mix
   (see page 10)
½ teaspoon ground cinnamon
¼ teaspoon ground ginger
¼ nutmeg, grated
1 quantity 50/50 coating
   (see page 10)

METHOD

Soak the sultanas in the rum overnight or until plump. Drain the sultanas, retaining the rum. Make the marshmallow following the method on page 10. At Step 6, add 3 tablespoons of the reserved rum. Whisk the mix back to its original volume. This may take 5–10 minutes. Add the spices and sultanas. Scrape into a lightly greased baking tin to set. Once set, cut into cubes and dust with the 50/50 coating mix.

Makes about 20 large marshmallows

ALCOHOL-FREE VERSION

Soak the sultanas in 6 tablespoons orange juice instead of rum.

GIN & TONIC MARSHMALLOWS

These make a great first step into the world of more unusual marshmallow flavours. They guarantee a '. . . these really taste like a gin and tonic' response. The natural botanical taste of the gin is boosted by the extra juniper.

INGREDIENTS

3 juniper berries
100 ml (3 ½ fl oz) tonic water
1 quantity ingredients for vanilla
  marshmallow mix (see page 10)
2 tablespoons gin
1 quantity 50/50 coating (see page 10)
About 10 thin cucumber slices

METHOD

Crush the juniper berries in a mortar and pestle and place them in a small saucepan with the tonic water. Heat gently until the tonic water has reduced down to about one-third of its original volume. Remove the juniper berries and leave to cool.

Make the marshmallow mix following the method on page 10. As the final step before setting, add the gin and the reduced tonic water. Whisk the mix back up to its original volume. This may take 5–10 minutes of whisking until the mixture thickens again as the gelatine sets. Then scrape it out and leave to set in a lightly greased baking tin.

When it has set, cut into cubes and dust with the 50/50 coating mix. Serve each marshmallow with a thin slice of cucumber on the top.

Makes about 20 large marshmallows

ALCOHOL-FREE VERSION

Leaving the gin out of this recipe creates a delicious botanical marshmallow. An equal quantity of puréed cucumber could be added instead of the gin to heighten the fresh taste.

MARSHMALLOW VODKA

This is less of a recipe, more of a progression from sweet treat to indulgent adult drink. Start with classic vanilla marshmallows as the basis for this, but try your favourite flavoured ones too.

INGREDIENTS

10 large vanilla-flavoured
  marshmallows
240 ml (8 fl oz) vodka

METHOD

Chop the marshmallows into 1.25-cm (½-in) pieces and shake in a colander to remove excess coating. Put in a Kilner or other airtight jar and pour vodka over the top. Place the lid on the jar and leave to infuse for 48 hours in the fridge. Some or all of the marshmallows may have dissolved. You'll be left with a cloudy mix. Line a colander with fine muslin. Place the colander over a bowl and pour the infused vodka into it. Pour the vodka into a bottle and store in the fridge. Serve ice cold or use in your favourite cocktail.

BEER MARSHMALLOWS

Choose a substantial beer for this one. Frothy pale lagers won't have the depth of flavour to come alive in the marshmallow. You want something dark and earthy. Eat with salty snacks.

INGREDIENTS

5 sheets (8 g/¼ oz)
  platinum-strength leaf
  gelatine
400 ml (13 ½ fl oz) ale
1 teaspoon vegetable oil
1 egg white (35 g/1 ¼ oz)
300 g (10 oz) caster sugar
1 ½ tablespoons glucose
  syrup
1 teaspoon vanilla extract
1 quantity 50/50 coating
  (see page 10)

METHOD

Make the marshmallow mix following the method on page 10, but with the following changes: Instead of softening the gelatine in water, bloom the sheets in 300 ml (10 fl oz) of the ale and use 4 tablespoons of the ale in place of the water for the sugar syrup. Add the remaining ale to the marshmallow mix during the final stages of whisking. This may take 5–10 minutes of whisking until the mixture thickens again as the gelatine sets. Spread into a greased baking tin and leave to set. Cut into cubes and dust with 50/50 coating mix.

Makes about 20 large marshmallows

STOUT MARSHMALLOWS

Follow the recipe, but replace the ale with Irish stout and add natural black food colouring. Make a quarter batch of vanilla marshmallow mix and spread over the top. When set, cut out circles to recreate the just-served pint effect.

MARSHMALLOWTINI

Despite its frivolous sweet base, this is a really sensible and refined drink. Decorated with split vanilla beans, it's as elegant as it is delightful.

INGREDIENTS

3 tablespoons marshmallow vodka (see page 70)
1 tablespoon Grand Marnier
1 tablespoon sugar syrup (see tip below)
1 vanilla bean
Ice cubes

METHOD

Mix all the ingredients other than the vanilla bean in a cocktail shaker or small jug. Stir gently and then strain into a martini glass.

Split the vanilla bean down its length. Cut a small lengthwise strip and rest it in the drink.

Serves 1

TIP

Sugar syrup is made by heating equal quantities by weight of sugar and water until the sugar dissolves.

EGG NOG MARSHMALLOWS

If we're honest, no one actually enjoys egg nog, but take those flavours and combine them with a marshmallow and they become a delicious and perfect Christmas gift.

INGREDIENTS

1 quantity ingredients for vanilla marshmallow mix
   (see page 10)
2 vanilla beans
3 tablespoons brandy
½ nutmeg, grated
Natural yellow food colouring
50 g (1 ¾ oz) glacé cherries, chopped (optional)
1 quantity 50/50 coating (see page 10)

METHOD

Make the marshmallow mix following the method on page 10. Split the vanilla beans and add the seeds at Step 6. After the final whisking, add in the brandy, half the nutmeg and a few drops of the colouring. This may take 5–10 minutes of whisking until the mixture thickens again as the gelatine sets. Fold through the cherries (if using).

Scrape out the mix and set in a lightly greased baking tin. Once set, cut into cubes, stars, Christmas trees or other suitable festive shapes and dust with the 50/50 coating mix. Sprinkle with the remaining nutmeg – delicious served in hot chocolate.

Makes about 30 marshmallows

ALCOHOL-FREE VERSION

This recipe can be adjusted to make an alcohol-free version by omitting the brandy and adding in the glacé cherries.

Chapter 6

ADVENTUROUS

Take your taste buds on a trip around the world or liven up a cocktail party with marshmallow canapés. Exciting combinations include chipotle and black cardamom or chorizo, pimentón and lemon; try the classic crisp flavours of blue cheese and onion or even salt and vinegar.

CHORIZO, PIMENTÓN & LEMON MARSHMALLOWS

Hola, Señor Marshmallow! The sweet, spicy chorizo works fabulously here. Little nuggets of savoury pork goodness stud the soft, spicy marshmallow while lemon juice balances the sweetness.

INGREDIENTS

75 g (3 oz) chorizo
1 quantity ingredients for vanilla marshmallow mix
  (see page 10)
½ teaspoon pimentón
Zest of 1 lemon
Juice of ½ lemon
1 quantity 50/50 coating (see page 10)

METHOD

Finely chop the chorizo or blend in a food processor for about 30 seconds.

Make the marshmallow mix following the method on page 10. At the final whisking stage, add in the pimentón, lemon zest and juice. The fat in the chorizo will cause the marshmallow to deflate a little, so add that in by folding through quickly just before scraping out the mix into a lightly greased baking tin to set.

Once set, cut into chunks and dust with the 50/50 coating mix. Serve as a part of a mind-blowing Spanish tapas adventure.

Makes 30 marshmallows

ROASTED CHIPOTLE & BLACK CARDAMOM MARSHMALLOWS

This is more about deep smoky flavours than blow-your-head-off chili spicing. Black cardamom is a remarkable spice that works here as a powerhouse of smoked awesomeness.

INGREDIENTS

5 dried chipotle chilis
3 black cardamom pods
1 quantity ingredients for vanilla
    marshmallow mix (see page 10)
1 quantity 50/50 coating (see page 10)

METHOD

Split the chilis and remove the seeds. Press them out flat. Heat a grill pan over high heat and place the flattened chilis on it. Cook them for 4–5 minutes until lightly browned, but be careful not to burn them.

Pour 180 ml (6 fl oz) cold water into a bowl. Place the chilis in the bowl and leave them to rehydrate for an hour or until soft. Drain the chilis but keep the water. Finely chop the chilis.

Crush the black cardamom pods and put in a small saucepan with the chili-infused water. Place over medium heat and bring to the simmer. Reduce the water to approximately one-third of its original volume. Leave the water and cardamom pods to infuse in the saucepan for 30 minutes. Remove the cardamom pods and discard.

Make the marshmallow mix following the method on page 10. Add the finely chopped chili and the chili- and cardamom-infused water at the final stage of whisking. Scrape out and leave to set in a lightly greased baking tin.

Once set, cut the marshmallows and dust with the 50/50 coating mix.

Makes 30 marshmallows

MATCHA GREEN TEA MARSHMALLOWS

Matcha should be the sixth taste: salt, sweet, sour, bitter, umami and 'matchary'. A grassy, puréed sensation – in the best and most wonderful sense. Matched by a green colour that can't be beaten. The sweetness of the marshmallow tempers the natural tannins and bitterness of the matcha. This is one of the best ways to try matcha if you haven't. Make 'em, sunshine.

INGREDIENTS
1 tablespoon matcha green tea powder, plus extra
    for dusting
1 quantity ingredients for vanilla marshmallow mix
    (see page 10)
1 quantity 50/50 coating (see page 10)

METHOD
Put the matcha powder in a bowl and mix to a paste with 3 tablespoons water.

Make the marshmallow mix following the method on page 10, adding the matcha paste during the final whisking. Whisk until combined and a deep green colour. Scrape out the marshmallow mix and set in a lightly greased baking tin.

Once set, cut and dust with the 50/50 coating mix and the matcha green tea powder.

Makes 30 large marshmallows

SPICED CARROT SOUP WITH TOASTED CORIANDER MARSHMALLOWS

Inspired by the American Thanksgiving classic of sweet potatoes and marshmallows, here is a warming soup studded with fragrant, spiced marshmallows. Their sweetness heightens the carrot flavour and proves again that the only thing better than a marshmallow is a melted marshmallow.

For the coriander marshmallows:
75 g (3 oz) icing sugar
75 g (3 oz) cornflour
2 teaspoons ground coriander
3 tablespoons coriander seeds
1 ½ egg whites (45 g/1 ¾ oz)
360 g (12 ¾ oz) caster sugar
2 tablespoons glucose syrup
13 sheets (22 g/⅞ oz) platinum-strength
    leaf gelatine, soaked in cold water
    until soft

For the spiced carrot soup:
1 tablespoon vegetable oil
500 g (1 lb 1 ½ oz) carrots,
    coarsely chopped
1 onion, coarsely chopped
1 stick celery, chopped
Thumb-size piece of fresh ginger,
    sliced (unpeeled)
2 teaspoons ground coriander
1 star anise
About 1 litre (33 fl oz) vegetable stock
    (made from a bouillon cube or powder
    is fine)
½ bunch of coriander, chopped

METHOD

To make the marshmallows, line a baking tin with wax paper. Combine the icing sugar, cornflour and ground coriander in a small bowl and lightly dust the lined baking tin with a little of the mixture.

Put the coriander seeds in a small dry frying pan over moderate heat and toast until the fragrance from the seeds is released. Tip out and crush coarsely with the back of knife or mortar and pestle. Place the crushed seeds in a small saucepan with 5 tablespoons water and heat until it boils. Remove from the heat and infuse for 30 minutes. Strain the water into a measuring cup and add cold water to return the volume to 5 tablespoons.

Place the egg whites in the bowl of a free-standing mixer. A hand-held electric mixer will also work. Mix the coriander water, caster sugar and glucose syrup in a medium saucepan and heat, measuring the temperature of the syrup with a digital sugar thermometer. As the temperature gets close to 120°C (250°F) start to whisk the egg white. When 120°C (250°F) is reached, pour the sugar syrup onto the egg white and continue to whisk until stiff peaks have formed.

Meanwhile, squeeze the residual water from the gelatine sheets. While the egg white is still whisking, gently melt the softened gelatine in a small saucepan over very low heat.

Pour the liquid gelatine onto the egg white and sugar syrup. Whisk back up to soft peaks.

Scrape the warm marshmallow mix into the dusted baking tin and dust the top with more of the icing sugar, cornflour and coriander mix. Leave to set overnight.

Once set, chop the marshmallows into small 1.25-cm (½-in) cubes, dusting each cube again with the remaining coriander coating.

To make the carrot soup, heat the oil in a large saucepan and add the chopped vegetables and the ginger. Cook for 10 minutes over medium heat until softened. Add the ground coriander and star anise and cook for an additional 5 minutes.

Pour over 475 ml (16 fl oz) of the vegetable stock and bring to the boil. Simmer until the carrot is just soft. Remove the star anise and then purée with an immersion blender. Add the remaining stock until you have the consistency desired.

Pour the soup into small bowls and sprinkle with the marshmallows and chopped coriander.

Serves 6

BLUE CHEESE & ONION MARSHMALLOWS

In the same way you'd eat cheese with sweet pickle or fruit, cheese in a marshmallow is not so strange. You need a bold and brave cheese – a punchy blue one is perfect. Not convinced? Well, they are coated in crispy onions and everything covered in crispy onions is tasty. Fact.

INGREDIENTS

1 quantity ingredients for vanilla
   marshmallow mix (see page 10)
75 g (3 oz) blue cheese, finely crumbled
Vegetable oil for frying
2 onions, finely sliced

METHOD

Make the marshmallow mix following the method on page 10. Just before scraping out the mix to set, add the blue cheese. The fat in the cheese will cause the mix to collapse dramatically if you mix it too much. Add it quickly, stir it through, then quickly tip out into a lightly greased baking tin to set.

Fill a large saucepan with vegetable oil to a depth of 1.25 cm (½ in) and place over medium heat. Add the onions in batches and fry until golden and crispy. Remove from the oil with a slotted spoon and drain on paper towels. Leave to cool, then chop into small pieces that are still big enough to give some crunch.

Once set, cut the marshmallows into chunks and coat in the crispy onions. These marshmallows won't keep well and are best made and eaten on the same day.

Makes 20 large marshmallows

TEMPURA MARSHMALLOWS

There's a bit of a knack to getting these to work. You'll need larger marshmallows and will have to freeze them before frying. Otherwise, the marshmallow disappears into the oil, lost forever. You'll be left with batter and a sense of emptiness.

INGREDIENTS

Your favourite marshmallows
Ice-cold sparkling mineral water
150 g (5 ½ oz) tempura batter mix,
   or 60 g (2 oz) cornflour, 100 g (3 ½ oz) plain
   flour and 2 teaspoons baking powder

Vegetable oil for deep-frying
Icing sugar for dusting

METHOD

Place the marshmallows in the freezer overnight.

Add enough cold sparkling water to either the batter mix or the combined cornflour, flour and baking powder to create a thick batter.

Half fill a large, deep saucepan with vegetable oil and heat to 180°C (350°F).

Coat the frozen marshmallows in the batter and carefully drop the marshmallows into the hot oil. Fry for 10 seconds. Dust with icing sugar and eat immediately.

Makes 15–18 marshmallows

SALT & VINEGAR MARSHMALLOWS

Stay with me on this one. If any of these more adventurous recipes need trying, it's this one. Perhaps 'vinegar' is misleading since what you need here is a syrupy sweet, tangy balsamic, not what you sprinkle over your fish and chips. Great as a canapé, the deep black colour will intrigue and delight your guests.

INGREDIENTS

1 quantity ingredients for vanilla marshmallow mix
  (see page 10)
1 tablespoon balsamic vinegar
¾ teaspoon fine table salt
Natural black food colouring
1 quantity 50/50 coating (see page 10)

METHOD

Make the marshmallow mix following the method on page 10, adding the vinegar, salt and enough black food colouring to give a deep, black colour during the final whisking. Check the seasoning and add more salt or vinegar if desired.

Scrape the mix into a lightly greased baking tin to set. Once set, cut into perfect cubes and dust with the 50/50 coating mix.

Makes 30 marshmallows

TIP

Try using coarser sea salt or kosher salt as it gives a better taste, but ensure you've ground it down finely before adding it to the mix.

PORCINI MARSHMALLOWS

These achieve a powerful mushroom taste in a small mouthful. If you're feeling super extravagant, a grating of fresh truffle would raise their game still further. As tasty as these are eaten alone, they work really well melted into other dishes. A few tucked inside a baked potato or dropped into a soup would be wonderful.

INGREDIENTS

25 g (1 oz) dried porcini mushrooms
1 quantity ingredients for vanilla
   marshmallow mix (see page 10)
1 tablespoon Worcestershire sauce
1 quantity 50/50 coating (see page 10)
1 teaspoon truffle honey (optional)

METHOD

Place all but a few of the dried porcini mushrooms in a bowl and pour in just enough hot water to cover. Put the remaining porcini mushrooms in a spice grinder and blend to a fine powder or grate with a fine Microplane grater.

When the soaked porcini are soft, finely chop them or purée them in a blender.

Make the marshmallow mix following the method on page 10, adding the finely ground dried mushrooms, chopped soaked mushrooms and Worcestershire sauce at the final whisking stage. Scrape into a lightly greased baking tin and leave to set.

Once set, chop into cubes or cut with a mushroom-shaped biscuit cutter. Dust with the 50/50 coating mix. For added decadence, drizzle with a little truffle honey before serving.

Makes 20 large marshmallows

MARMITE & PRETZEL MARSHMALLOWS

Salty, savoury, crunchy and delicious. The sweetness of the marshmallow rounds off the edges of the spiky-tasting Marmite. Cut these smaller than usual since you'll want lots of coating crunch to balance the softer marshmallow. These are best consumed with a cold beer, watching sport on TV.

INGREDIENTS

1 quantity ingredients for vanilla marshmallow mix (see page 10)
1 tablespoon Marmite (see tip below)
100 g (3 ½ oz) pretzels (the small crunchy snack, not its bigger bread cousin)

METHOD

Make the marshmallow mix following the method on page 10. Just before scraping the marshmallow mix out to set, add the Marmite and whisk it in. You may want to start with ½ tablespoon then add more to taste.

Scrape out the marshmallow mix into a lightly greased baking tin and leave to set.

Crush the pretzels in the bag or a bowl until you have small 2–3 mm ($\frac{1}{10}$–$\frac{1}{8}$-in) pieces. Cut the marshmallow into small 2-cm ($\frac{3}{4}$-in) pieces and toss in the pretzels to coat.

Makes 30 small marshmallows

TIP

Vegemite, Bovril and other umami hot spots work just as well as Marmite. At a stretch, a bouillon cube made into a paste with a bit of water would do the trick.

Chapter 7

PARTY

Make a birthday, wedding or just a good day at the office extra special
with a marshmallow-studded cake or dessert. From frostings and sundae
sauces, to Rice Krispie treats and pecan pie bark, there are plenty of
options for sweet-toothed celebrations.

MARSHMALLOW POPCORN

Marshmallows and popcorn are best friends, Mrs Marshmallow softening Mr Popcorn's crunchiness. These are best made and eaten while still warm, served in a big bowl on the couch.

INGREDIENTS

2 tablespoons canola or vegetable oil
75 g (3 oz) popping corn
75 g (3 oz) butter
75 g (3 oz) brown sugar
2 handfuls of vanilla marshmallows (see page 10)
¼ teaspoon sea salt

METHOD

Heat the oil in a large saucepan with a lid. Tip in the popcorn and stir briefly to coat the corn in oil. Cover and keep the tin on moderate heat until the corn starts popping. Turn the heat off and let the magic happen.

Melt the butter in a saucepan over medium heat. Add the brown sugar and the marshmallows and stir until smooth. Add the salt.

Pour the buttery, sugary marshmallow goodness over the popped corn and stir until the corn is well coated.

These will harden up over time and, if kept in an airtight container, will be good for 2–3 days.

Makes about 11 cups

MARSHMALLOW CHOCOLATE PECAN PIE BARK

This is a wonderful sweet sandwich. Perhaps it is best eaten in small pieces, but none the less, it ticks all the sweet, salty, chocolate, caramel and marshmallow boxes. Oh, and pecans too.

INGREDIENTS

400 g (13 oz) milk chocolate
1 quantity vanilla marshmallows
   (see page 10)
225 g (8 oz) caster sugar
60 g (2 oz) butter
120 ml (4 fl oz) double cream
¼ teaspoon salt
150 g (5 ½ oz) pecans

METHOD

Line a 20-cm (8-in) square baking tin with wax paper.

Melt the chocolate in a heat-proof bowl set over a saucepan of barely simmering water (bain-marie or double-boiler). Pour half the chocolate into the lined baking tin and smooth with an offset spatula. Leave to set.

Melt the marshmallows in a small saucepan over low heat. Pour the melted marshmallow over the set chocolate and leave that layer to set.

Make the caramel sauce by heating the caster sugar in a dry saucepan over medium heat. Watch the sugar all the time and stir it with a spoon to melt it evenly. Yes, it's okay to stir the sugar – with this method it won't crystallise if stirred. When the sugar has melted to a light brown caramel, add the butter and cream. At this point the caramel will spit. Be careful.

Continue to stir over medium heat and the crystallised sugar will melt away. Once all the sugar has melted and the sauce is smooth, cook for an additional 2 minutes. Add the salt and leave to cool.

Sprinkle the pecans over the marshmallow and pour the caramel over the top. Place in the fridge until the caramel is firm. Reheat the remaining chocolate and pour over the top of the caramel and nuts. Leave to set completely. Then remove from the tray and break into pieces.

Makes 30 marshmallows

MARSHMALLOW & PISTACHIO CHOCOLATE FUDGE

Bejeweled with pistachios and marshmallows, this fudge would make a great gift gathered into clear plastic gift bags and tied with ribbon. This is a fudgy fudge, not a grainy fudge – the glucose and the chocolate see to that.

INGREDIENTS

140 g (4 ½ oz) milk chocolate
480 ml (16 fl oz) double cream
500 g (1 lb 1 ½ oz) caster sugar
4 ½ tablespoons glucose syrup
150 g (5 ½ oz) shelled pistachios
2 handfuls of vanilla marshmallows (see page 10),
   chopped into 2.5-cm (½-in) cubes

METHOD

Lightly grease a 20-cm (8-in) square tin.

Melt the chocolate in a heat-proof bowl set over a saucepan of barely simmering water (bain-marie or double-boiler). Keep the chocolate warm and molten.

Put the cream, sugar and glucose syrup in a saucepan and stir together over medium heat. Stir continuously and measure the temperature. When the mixture reaches 118°C (244°F), remove from the heat and stir in the melted chocolate. Then add the nuts and pour into the greased pan. Leave the fudge to cool a little, then sprinkle with the marshmallow cubes. You need it at a temperature that doesn't melt the marshmallows too much but does let them stick to the top of the fudge.

Leave to set fully, then cut into squares and serve.

Makes 30 pieces

MARSHMALLOW SKEWERS

The fun here is the construction. Perfect as a children's birthday party activity, these might be best scheduled for the end of the party so the chocolate- and sprinkle-covered, sticky-fingered guests can be propelled quickly into the arms of delighted parents.

INGREDIENTS

400 g (13 oz) plain chocolate
1 quantity vanilla marshmallows
(see page 10)

For the coatings:
Finely chopped hazelnuts
Chocolate sprinkles
Pop rocks
Ice-cream sprinkles

Water icing (icing sugar and water mixed to
a pipeable paste)

Wooden skewers

METHOD

Melt the chocolate in a heat-proof bowl set over a saucepan of barely simmering water (bain-marie or double-boiler) and stir gently until melted.

Place the bowl of melted chocolate in the middle of a well-protected table. Slide the marshmallows onto wooden skewers, then dunk into the chocolate.

Place the coatings in small bowls and sprinkle over the marshmallows. Leave the skewers to set. They can be held up to dry and harden by pushing the ends of the skewers into a Styrofoam box or a melon cut in half and placed cut-side down on a dish.

Put the water icing into a piping bag with a small (1-mm/$\frac{1}{16}$-in) round tip. Decorate and drizzle the coated marshmallows.

Makes 6–8 skewers

STUFFED BEURRE NOISETTE MARSHMALLOW RICE KRISPIE CAKES

Hold onto your hats, this is a Rice Krispie treat that is an 11 out of 10 on the flavour scale – proving again the amazing effect beurre noisette has on cakes and the versatility of marshmallow as an ingredient.

INGREDIENTS

1 ½ quantities ingredients for vanilla marshmallow mix (see page 10)
1 ½ teaspoons vanilla extract
50 g (1 ¾ oz) butter
¼ teaspoon salt
200 g (7 oz) Rice Krispies

METHOD

Lightly grease two 30 x 20-cm (12 x 8-in) baking tins.

Make the marshmallow mix following the method on page 10 and flavour with the vanilla at step 6. During the final whisking stage, start to melt the butter in a large saucepan. Continue to heat until the butter foams and starts to turn a light brown colour. Remove the saucepan from the heat.

Remove two-thirds of the marshmallow mix from the mixer bowl and stir into the brown butter. Add the salt and stir the mix until smooth. Add in the Rice Krispies and stir until well combined. Put half of the Krispie mix into each pan. Place in the fridge to set firm. Keep the remaining marshmallow mix to one side. It will set but that's okay.

Once the mix has set, remove one of the sheets of Rice Krispie cake from the baking tin and set aside. Warm up the remaining one-third marshmallow mix by placing the bowl over a saucepan of simmering water and stirring until loose and smooth. Tip this onto the Rice Krispie cake in its tin and press the other cake on top.

Leave the whole thing to set again and then cut into squares. Scrumptious.

Makes 16 squares

MARSHMALLOW RICE KRISPIE CAKES

This is the never-fails-to-please children's party classic. A classic because, like all the best children's party food, it's most enjoyed by adults. Make more than you need. They'll get eaten.

INGREDIENTS

50 g (1 ¾ oz) butter
1 quantity vanilla marshmallows
  (see page 10)
200 g (7 oz) Rice Krispies

METHOD

Lightly grease a 30 x 20-cm (12 x 8-in) baking tin.

Melt the butter in a large saucepan over medium heat. Once melted, add the marshmallows and stir until dissolved and you have a smooth sauce. Remove the saucepan from the heat.

Tip the Rice Krispies into the butter and marshmallow mix and stir well. Spoon the mix into the prepared baking tin. Press it down with the back of a large spoon until well compacted. Yes, it will be sticky, but lick your fingers.

Leave to cool until hard then remove from the tin and cut into squares.

Makes 16 squares

MARSHMALLOW CHOCOLATE CHIP COOKIE SANDWICHES

Ooh-la-la, these are tasty. Using the same principle as ice-cream sandwiches, here dense and chewy chocolate chip biscuits are sandwiched together with soft marshmallow. The advantage is that they won't melt so easily and can be kept in lunch boxes and bags for covert eating. Try constructing them while the biscuits are still warm. Eaten just after filling, they are scrumptious.

INGREDIENTS

50 g (1 ¾ oz) caster sugar
50 g (1 ¾ oz) light brown sugar
125 g (4 ½ oz) butter (at room temperature)
1 egg
½ teaspoon vanilla extract
½ teaspoon salt
225 g (8 oz) self-raising flour
180 g (6 oz) milk chocolate
½ quantity ingredients for vanilla
    marshmallow mix (see page 10)

METHOD

Preheat the oven to 200°C (400°F). Line two baking trays with parchment paper.

Cream together the sugars and the butter in a large bowl until pale and fluffy. Add the egg and beat until smooth. Add the vanilla and salt, then fold in the flour. Chop the chocolate into coarse chunks no bigger than 1.25 cm (½ in).

Using a medium ice-cream scoop, make round mounds of dough and evenly space them on the baking trays. Flatten them a little with your hand. Bake in the oven for 8–10 minutes until the edges are starting to brown but the centres are still soft.

While the biscuits bake, make the vanilla marshmallow mix following the method on page 10. When the biscuits are done, spoon or pipe the marshmallow onto the flat base of one biscuit. Fill generously, there's no harm in the marshmallow oozing out a little. Place another biscuit on top. EAT!

Makes 7–8 biscuit sandwiches

SALTED CARAMEL MARSHMALLOW TEACAKES

Here is a cheeky little twist on the British teatime classic. Sometimes it's hard not to add salted caramel to everything, but here that salt helps to cut through what's otherwise a rather sweet cake. Making these is a bit tricky, but one bite and you'll know it was all worthwhile.

For the biscuits:
25 g (1 oz) butter
25 g (1 oz) caster sugar
Pinch of salt
100 g (3 ½ oz) plain flour
1 tablespoon milk

For the salted caramel sauce:
50 g (1 ¾ oz) caster sugar
100 ml (3 ½ fl oz) double cream
25 g (1 oz) butter
½ teaspoon sea salt

400 g (13 oz) plain chocolate
1 quantity vanilla marshmallow frosting
   (see page 106)
Silicone demisphere mould with a sphere
   diameter of 7 cm (2 ¾ in)
   (see Resources, page 144)

METHOD

Line a baking tray with parchment paper.

To make the biscuits, cream the butter and sugar together in a bowl. Add the salt and flour and mix together with your hands or in a free-standing mixer. Add the milk and work the dough into a smooth ball. Cover with cling film and chill in the fridge for an hour.

Roll out the dough on a floured work surface to about 3 mm (⅛ in) thick. Cut out six 7-cm (2 ¾-in) round biscuits and place on the lined baking tray. Refrigerate the biscuits again for 1 hour.

Preheat the oven to 160°C (325°F). Bake the biscuits from chilled for 9–10 minutes until firm and an even brown colour. Leave to cool.

The chocolate coating is ideally made from tempered chocolate. The detail of how to do that is beyond the scope of this book, but there are excellent videos on the technique online. If not tempering, melt the chocolate in a heat-proof bowl placed over a saucepan of barely simmering water (bain-marie or double-boiler). Leave the chocolate to cool and thicken slightly and then coat the insides of the demispheres with an even layer of the chocolate. This won't require all the chocolate. Reserve the remaining chocolate and leave the chocolate-coated moulds to cool.

To make the salted caramel sauce, place the caster sugar in a medium saucepan and heat gently over moderate heat. Move the sugar around the saucepan by gently tipping it. It's okay to stir the caramel with this method if it's melting unevenly. As soon as it has turned a light brown colour, pour in the cream and butter. This creates lots of steam and fussing in the saucepan. The caramel will seize and look awful, but keep stirring and the sugar will melt back into the cream. Once it has all melted and is smooth, cook on moderate heat for 2 minutes or until thickened slightly. Add the salt and leave to cool.

Make the marshmallow frosting following the method on page 106.

To construct the teacakes, pipe or spoon a teaspoon of salted caramel sauce into the bottom of each chocolate-coated mould. Then pipe in the marshmallow frosting to just below the surface.

Warm the reserved chocolate. Dunk one side of a biscuit in the chocolate then press that side onto the marshmallow. Use any remaining chocolate to seal and neaten the join between biscuit, marshmallow and chocolate dome. Repeat for each of the cakes. Leave the complete teacakes to set.

Carefully demould and admire your hard work.

Makes 6

GRAND MARSHMALLOW WEDDING CAKE

You're going to need a lot of marshmallows, but the effect is impressive and far more fun and interesting than a sugar paste-covered fruit cake. The marshmallows can be made over a week or two and stored in airtight containers until construction.

INGREDIENTS

Styrofoam tower
Food-safe tissue paper
Lots of cocktail sticks
Lots of marshmallows (see tip below)

METHOD

Cover the tower with the food-safe tissue of your choice. Wrap it tightly and fix with small pieces of adhesive tape.

Starting at the bottom, push cocktail sticks into the tower then slide the marshmallows on. If you use alternating colours of marshmallows you'll slowly build a spiral effect as the marshmallows build.

The tower can be positioned on top of a more traditional cake if you want something to cut into. Construct the tower and place on a thin cake board. Dowel the cake so the tower's weight is supported and simply rest on top.

Decoration: These towers cry out for over-the-top decoration– think rose petals, candy canes, edible flowers, spirals of ribbon and sparklers in the top. A wedding cake for the young at heart.

TIP

Styrofoam towers come in many sizes. As a guide, if using plain round cut marshmallows 3 cm (1 ¼ in) in diameter:

- 20 cm (8 in) high, 9 cm (3 ½-in) diameter base – 40 marshmallows
- 30.5 cm (12 in) high, 11.5 cm (4 ¼-in) diameter base – 90 marshmallows
- 56 cm (22 in) high, 17 cm (6 ¾-in) diameter base – 170 marshmallows

The exact numbers you'll need will vary significantly depending on how closely you place the marshmallows.

BEURRE NOISETTE MARSHMALLOW SAUCE

Poured over your favourite baked treats such as brownies and waffles or drizzled over ice cream, this sauce is difficult to beat. The beurre noisette (brown butter) adds a complex nutty taste. It also brings a little French refinement.

INGREDIENTS

50 g (1 ¾ oz) butter
50 g (1 ¾ oz) caster sugar
275 ml (9 fl oz) double cream
2 handfuls of vanilla marshmallows
   (see page 10)

METHOD

Warm the butter in a small saucepan over medium heat. Leave it to melt and then froth. Watch it carefully. The butter will continue to froth and the foam will begin to turn a light brown colour. This is the point when the milk solids in the butter begin to caramelise. The butter will begin to smell nutty. At this point, remove from the heat and leave to cool a little.

The butter can be used in the sauce right away, but for a cleaner appearance, the milk solids at the bottom of the tin can be filtered out. Place a paper towel in a fine sieve and pass the butter through.

Return the filtered butter to the tin. Add the caster sugar to the warm butter and stir until dissolved. Add the cream and bring to the simmer. Toss in the marshmallows and stir until smooth and unctuous.

TIP

Obviously, different marshmallow flavours will give different flavoured sauces. Try salted caramel sauce with fresh waffles or triple chocolate marshmallows on vanilla ice cream. Boom!

SHERBET DIPPING MARSHMALLOWS

Sherbet is the best, right? At school we made sherbet fingers. It involved licking your finger and dipping it in sherbet. Licking your finger again, but leaving some sherbet . . . and repeat. You ended up with a sherbet-cocooned finger. Amazing. If that hasn't put you off for life – try these.

INGREDIENTS

1 quantity ingredients for vanilla
  marshmallow mix (see page 10)
50 g (1 ¾ oz) icing sugar
1 teaspoon citric acid
  (see Resources, page 144)
1 teaspoon bicarbonate of soda
Freeze-dried fruit powders – try raspberry,
  strawberry or blueberry (see Resources,
  page 144)

METHOD

Make the marshmallow mix following the method on page 10 and leave undusted. Cut out cubes.

In a small food processor or spice grinder, mix together the icing sugar, citric acid and bicarbonate of soda. This should give a fine dusty powder. Add 1 tablespoon fruit powder to the sherbet mix.

Dip the marshmallow into sherbet to coat half of it and eat.

Makes 30

CHOCOLATE ORANGE MELTED MARSHMALLOW FONDUE

Melting marshmallows into a warm chocolate sauce adds flavour but also a great stringy texture. To balance the rich sauce, you'll need to dunk in fresh juicy fruit . . . or, when no one's watching, use more marshmallows. The addition of orange zest also helps to lighten the sauce, but feel free to leave it out if that's not your thing.

INGREDIENTS

400 g (13 oz) milk chocolate
240 ml (8 fl oz) double cream
4 tablespoons milk
Zest of 1 large orange, finely grated
Fresh fruit to dip in – banana, strawberries and grapes
2 handfuls of vanilla marshmallows (see page 10)

METHOD

Break the chocolate into small pieces and put in a small saucepan with the cream and milk. Place over low heat. Stir gently until the chocolate has melted. Add the orange zest.

When ready to serve, prepare the fruit: slice bananas and cut any large strawberries in half. Warm the chocolate sauce. Seat your guests.

Toss the marshmallows into the melted chocolate sauce and stir until they begin to melt. Transfer the mix to a fondue pot before the marshmallows completely dissolve. Start dunking.

Serves 6

TOASTED MARSHMALLOW CLOTTED CREAM ICE CREAM

The smoky, burnt sugar taste of toasted marshmallow mixed through soft vanilla ice cream is a joy. Don't be afraid to really toast the marshmallows. Those crunchy brown sugar nuggets are ice cream gold. Combined with clotted cream, this is an extraordinary dessert.

INGREDIENTS

2 large eggs
2 egg yolks
150 g (5 ½ oz) caster sugar
240 ml (8 fl oz) double cream
240 ml (8 fl oz) milk
225 g (8 oz) clotted cream
2 handfuls of vanilla marshmallows
  (see page 10)

METHOD

Whisk together the whole eggs, egg yolks and sugar in a bowl. Put the double cream and milk in a saucepan and warm to just boiling.

Pour approximately one-quarter of the hot cream and milk onto the eggs and sugar and stir until smooth. Tip this mix back into the remaining cream and milk and warm gently, stirring until thickened. Remove from the heat and leave to cool in a clean bowl. Refrigerate until cold, then whisk through the clotted cream.

Line the marshmallows up on a baking tray. They can be either placed underneath a very hot grill and toasted or flamed with a kitchen torch. The marshmallows will puff up, some may catch fire. That's all good. When they are all nicely charred, scrape them up and blend them in a food processor.

Add the toasted marshmallow paste into the chilled ice-cream mix, pour into an ice-cream machine and churn until soft.

Serves 8

TIP

If you prefer, the ice cream can be churned first and the charred marshmallow pieces added toward the end to create small pockets of burned marshmallow excitement.

S'MORES ICE-CREAM SUNDAES

On a hot summer's day, what better than a dessert to remind you of the colder dark times around the corner? Soak up the sun and be thankful. These work particularly well if you use the toasted marshmallow clotted cream ice cream on page 103.

INGREDIENTS

For the chocolate sauce:
100 g (3 ½ oz) plain chocolate
25 g (1 oz) icing sugar
100 g (3 ½ oz) golden syrup
80 ml (2 ¾ fl oz) double cream
Pinch of salt

4 digestive biscuits
4 scoops vanilla or toasted marshmallow
   clotted cream ice cream (see page 103)
½ quantity vanilla marshmallow frosting
   (see page 106)
1 handful of vanilla marshmallows
   (see page 10)

METHOD

Make the chocolate sauce by breaking the chocolate in pieces and melting it in a heat-proof bowl set over a saucepan of barely simmering water (bain-marie or double-boiler). Once melted, stir in the sugar, syrup, cream and salt.

Crumble two biscuits into the bases of four sundae glasses or bowls. Scoop in half the ice cream on top of the crumbs. Pipe or spoon in half the marshmallow frosting, then drizzle with a little of the chocolate sauce. Tumble in some marshmallows. Add the remaining ice cream and marshmallow frosting. Drizzle with more chocolate sauce and then add more biscuit crumbs on the top.

Position the remaining marshmallows on top of each sundae and use a kitchen torch to scorch the marshmallow to perfection. Eat with big spoons and gusto.

Serves 4

VANILLA MARSHMALLOW FROSTING

This voluminous creamy delight isn't a marshmallow in the 'set with gelatine' sense but certainly recreates that fluffy effect. It's where marshmallow meets meringue. The egg whites are cooked with the sugar in a bain-marie or double-boiler and then stabilised with the cream of tartar.

INGREDIENTS

6 medium egg whites (210 g/7 ½ oz)
360 g (12 ¾ oz) caster sugar
¼ teaspoon cream of tartar
Seeds from 2 vanilla beans or 1 teaspoon
   vanilla extract

METHOD

Place the egg whites and caster sugar in a heat-proof bowl. Ideally, use the bowl of your free-standing mixer as this will mean you don't have to transfer it for the final whisking. Rest the bowl over a saucepan of simmering water. Ensure the bottom of the bowl doesn't touch the water.

Whisk the egg whites and sugar continuously while measuring the temperature with a digital sugar thermometer. You need to reach a temperature of 61°C (143°F), which is the point at which the egg white is cooked. Remove from the tin and place in the free-standing mixer or begin to whisk with an electric handmixer.

Whisk to stiff peaks, then stir in the cream of tartar and the vanilla. Use immediately.

Makes enough to fill and frost a 20-cm (8-in) diameter cake

TIP

This meringue/marshmallow recipe works really well baked in a low oven. It gives a particularly dense and close structure that can be used to make meringue shapes and decorations. This should be your go-to recipe for meringue mushrooms and snowmen.

MARSHMALLOW BUTTERCREAM FROSTING

This is a simple way of incorporating new flavours into your favourite cakes. It takes a simple buttercream recipe and blends that with melted marshmallow. Change the marshmallow; change the flavour. It works particularly well if you add unmelted marshmallows as a decoration.

INGREDIENTS

120 g (4 ¼ oz) unsalted butter
240 g (8 ½ oz) icing sugar, sieved
1 tablespoon milk
2 handfuls marshmallows

METHOD

Beat the butter in a bowl until soft, then slowly add the sieved icing sugar. If you prefer, this can all be done in a food processor. Beat until smooth and then add the milk to loosen the mix a little.

Melt the marshmallows in a saucepan over low heat. You will need to stir them all the time. Almost certainly, some of the marshmallow will stick to the base of the saucepan. Once the marshmallow has melted, leave it to cool slightly. If it's too hot it will melt the butter and you'll have a sauce, not a frosting. When slightly cooled, beat the melted marshmallow into the buttercream and use to decorate sponge and cupcakes.

TIP

This will be the only time we mention it, but there is something called marshmallow fluff. It comes in a jar. Obviously, having read this book and made every recipe, you'll have come to appreciate that the world no longer requires this . . . fluff. However, if you used some here, instead of melting marshmallows, it would probably be acceptable and save a little time.

TOASTED MARSHMALLOW MILKSHAKES

These milky treats work well as a straightforward children's favourite or, with the addition of a little coffee liqueur, can be transformed into a much more exciting adult drink.

INGREDIENTS

5 large vanilla marshmallows (see page 10)
2 scoops vanilla ice cream
120 ml (4 fl oz) milk

METHOD

Scorch four of the marshmallows with a kitchen torch until charred, puffed and browned all over. Alternatively, place them under a hot grill for a few seconds until ready.

Put the ice cream and milk into a blender and scrape in the charred marshmallows. Blend until smooth. Pour into a tall glass and float the last marshmallow on the top. Scorch that marshmallow with the kitchen torch as it floats.

Serve with a stripy straw.

Serves 1

TIP

For an adult version, add 1 ½ tablespoons coffee liqueur (Kahlúa) before blending.

Chapter 8

CAKES & DESSERTS

We all know how good marshmallows taste in rocky road and s'mores, but they also add an extra dimension to many more classic cake and dessert recipes. Try them instead of the meringue on a lemon meringue pie, in brownies and blondies and to ice a carrot cake.

GROWN-UP ROCKY ROAD

Don't underestimate this classic. Think of the sweet chocolate and butter foundation as a canvas to be embroidered with delicious and exotic delights. Obviously, the marshmallows need pride of place, but use your imagination and add your sweet and nutty favourites.

INGREDIENTS

150 g (5 ½ oz) plain chocolate

7 oz (200 g) milk chocolate

75 g (3 oz) butter

1 tablespoon golden syrup

50 g (1 ¾ oz) shelled pistachios

1 handful of vanilla marshmallows (see page 10), chopped into 1.25-cm (½-in) cubes

4 pieces of crystallised ginger, coarsely chopped

4 tablespoons mixed peel

75 g (3 oz) biscuits, crushed into small pieces – try gingersnaps or digestives

METHOD

Line a 15-cm (6-in) square tin with overlapping sheets of cling film.

Melt the chocolates, butter and syrup together in a bowl placed over a saucepan of simmering water. Make sure the base of the bowl isn't touching the water.

When melted, remove from the heat and stir in the remaining ingredients. Push down into the lined tin and leave to set in the fridge.

When set, cut into squares.

Makes 30

TIPS

The appearance of Rocky Road can be heightened by setting it in different moulds. Using a bûche tin, as in the marshmallow bûche cake recipe on page 140, gives a more refined look. It is only rocky road, but a wisp or two of gold leaf decorating a slice wouldn't go amiss.

PBJ CARAMEL MARSHMALLOW BARS

This recipe is a distillation of guilty food pleasures and all the better for it. Freeze-dried fruit is available in supermarkets now and a great way of packing fruit flavour into cakes and biscuits.

INGREDIENTS

150 g (5 ½ oz) smooth peanut butter
100 g (3 ½ oz) butter
100 g (3 ½ oz) shelled peanuts
2 handfuls of vanilla marshmallows
    (see page 10), chopped into
    1.25-cm (½-in) cubes
10 g (¼ oz) freeze-dried raspberries
50 g (1 ¾ oz) caster sugar
100 ml (3 ½ fl oz) double cream
¼ teaspoon salt

METHOD

Melt the peanut butter and butter in a saucepan over low heat. Stir through the peanuts, marshmallows and raspberries. Press into the bottom of a 20-cm (8-in) square tin. Place the sugar in a small saucepan over medium heat. Stir with a spoon to help it melt and caramelise evenly. When it is a light brown colour, tip in the cream. It will spit, but ignore it and keep stirring. Stir continuously until you have a smooth, deep brown sauce. Add the salt. Drizzle over the peanut and marshmallow mix. Refrigerate the mix in the tin until firm. Cut into small squares.

Makes 30

CHOCOLATE MARSHMALLOW NUT BLONDIES

Using white chocolate creates a creamy rich vanilla blondie. The marshmallows act as a frosting. The macadamia nuts help balance the texture with some additional crunch.

INGREDIENTS

125 g (4 ½ oz) white chocolate
125 g (4 ½ oz) butter
2 eggs, beaten
225 g (8 oz) unrefined caster sugar
100 g (3 ½ oz) plain flour
½ teaspoon baking powder
100 g (3 ½ oz) macadamia nuts
2 handfuls of vanilla marshmallows,
    sliced (see page 10)

METHOD

Preheat the oven to 180°C (350°F). Line a 20-cm (8-in) square baking tin with silicone paper.

Melt the chocolate and butter in a heat-proof bowl over a saucepan of simmering water (bain-marie or double-boiler). Mix the eggs and sugar in a bowl – then mix through the chocolate and butter. Fold in the flour and baking powder. Add the nuts. Scrape into the prepared tin and level. Layer the sliced marshmallows over the blondie mix. Bake for 20 minutes. The mix should be set around the edge but still a little soft in the middle. Bake for a little longer if needed. Cool – then refrigerate in the tin overnight. Cut into squares.

Makes 30

MARSHMALLOW-CRUSTED BLUEBERRY MUFFINS

These are best eaten warm so the molten marshmallow and hot blueberries can work their magic on your palate. The toasted vanilla top adds textural contrast to the warm muffin underneath.

INGREDIENTS

200 g (7 oz) plain flour
60 g (2 oz) caster sugar
Pinch of salt
½ teaspoon bicarbonate of soda
2 teaspoons baking powder
75 g (3 oz) unsalted butter
180 ml (6 fl oz) buttermilk
1 egg
150 g (5 ½ oz) blueberries
24 large vanilla marshmallows (see page 10)

METHOD

Preheat the oven to 200°C (400°F). Combine the flour, sugar, salt, bicarbonate of soda and baking powder in a bowl. Melt the butter, then combine in another bowl with the buttermilk. Beat the egg and add to the buttermilk mixture.

Add the wet ingredients into the flour mixture and mix briefly. Don't overwork the batter. Stir in the blueberries. Spoon the batter into muffin cups. Push one whole marshmallow into the centre of each. Slice the remaining marshmallows and lay them over the top of the mix. Bake in the oven for 15–18 minutes or until well risen and golden.

Makes 12

CHOCOLATE MARSHMALLOW BROWNIES

The trick to these brownies is baking them properly. As with all brownies, it is better to underbake than overbake. Allowing the brownies to cool and then chilling them overnight creates a dense, fudgy texture.

INGREDIENTS

125 g (4 ½ oz) plain chocolate
125 g (4 ½ oz) butter
2 eggs, beaten
225 g (8 oz) brown sugar
125 g (4 ½ oz) plain flour
1 ½ tablespoons unsweetened cocoa powder
½ teaspoon baking powder
2 handfuls of vanilla marshmallows
  (see page 10)

METHOD

Preheat the oven to 180°C (350°F). Line a 20-cm (8-in) square baking tin with parchment paper.

Melt the chocolate and butter together in a heat-proof bowl over a saucepan of simmering water (bain-marie or double-boiler).

Mix together the eggs and sugar in a bowl then mix through the melted chocolate and butter. Fold in the flour, cocoa powder and baking powder.

Keep the marshmallows in large, approximately 2.5-cm (1-in), pieces and fold through the brownie mix.

Scrape the mix into the prepared baking tin and level. Bake in the oven for 20 minutes. Check them. The mix should be set around the edge but it's best if still a little soft in the middle. Bake for a little longer if needed. Remove from the oven and cool – then refrigerate the brownies in the tin overnight. Cut into squares.

Makes 30

WHITE CHOCOLATE & CARDAMOM MARSHMALLOW MOUSSE

Cardamom and white chocolate work wonderfully together. It scents the chocolate with intriguing lemony tones, making a grown-up and complex dessert that's brilliantly quick and simple to make. The marshmallow acts as an egg white substitute that both sweetens and lightens the mousse.

INGREDIENTS

8 plump cardamom pods
3 tablespoons milk
225 g (8 oz) white chocolate
2 handfuls of vanilla marshmallows
  (see page 10), chopped into
  1.25-cm (½-in) cubes
60 g (2 oz) butter
300 ml (10 fl oz) double cream

METHOD

Crush the cardamom pods to release the seeds and place them in a small saucepan with the milk. Gently warm the milk until it just starts to boil. Remove from the heat and leave to infuse for 1 hour. Strain the milk through a fine sieve and set aside.

Chop the chocolate and place with the marshmallows and butter in a heat-proof bowl over a saucepan of simmering water (bain-marie or double-boiler). When they have melted, add the infused milk. Stir until smooth and then Leave to cool a little.

Whisk the cream to soft peaks, then fold in the white chocolate mix. Spoon into individual glasses or one large serving bowl. Refrigerate.

Serves 6

CHOCOLATE CHIP MARSHMALLOW MACARONS

I couldn't resist this recipe. It's a mix of highfalutin' French patisserie and common biscuit sandwich. It succeeds or fails on how well the components contrast. Macaron shells require patience to get right, but once perfected, you'll have an impressive skill up your sleeve.

INGREDIENTS

200 g (7 oz) ground almonds
200 g (7 oz) icing sugar
4–5 (150 g/5 ½ oz) egg whites
200 g (7 oz) caster sugar
Unsweetened cocoa powder
   for dusting
½ quantity ingredients for vanilla
   marshmallow mix (see page 10)
100 g (3 ½ oz) plain chocolate chips

METHOD

Preheat the oven to 150°C (300°F). Line a baking tray with silicone paper. Combine the almonds, icing sugar and half the egg white in a bowl. Mix well until you have a thick paste.

Mix the caster sugar and 3 tablespoons water in a saucepan. Stir until the consistency of wet sand. Put the remaining egg white in the bowl of a free-standing mixer or use a bowl and a hand-held electric mixer. Heat the sugar and water to create a syrup. While the sugar syrup is heating, whisk the egg white to soft peaks. When the sugar syrup reaches 117°C (243°F) on a digital sugar thermometer, pour onto the egg white and whisk until it forms stiff peaks.

Combine this meringue with the ground almonds and icing sugar paste. Beat together slowly for 30 seconds then scrape down the sides of the bowl with a spatula and beat again for 30 seconds. The mix should flow smoothly and, when dropped back into the bowl, it should spread and form a flat even surface.

Transfer to a piping bag fitted with a 1.25-cm (½-in) plain round tip. Pipe twenty 8.25-cm (3 ¼-in) circles onto the lined baking tray. Dust lightly with cocoa powder. Place in the oven and turn it off. After 10 minutes, turn the heat to 150°C (300°F) and bake for 10 minutes. Remove from the oven and leave to cool on the sheet. Peel the shells off the parchment paper and pair up equal-size shells.

Make the vanilla marshmallow mix following the method on page 10. Pipe onto half the macaron shells and sprinkle with chocolate chips. Sandwich a second macaron shell on top and leave to set.

Makes 10

BAKED S'MORES

Avoid those marshmallows falling-off-the-fork-into-the-bonfire disasters or molten-chocolate-running-down-your-arm catastrophes. Let's face it, making s'mores can be a traumatic business – and perhaps only 1 in 10 works perfectly. Your problems are solved: make these and relax.

INGREDIENTS

100 g (3 ½ oz) light brown sugar
125 g (4 ½ oz) butter, room temperature
½ teaspoon vanilla extract
1 egg
½ teaspoon salt
225 g (8 oz) self-raising flour
200 g (7 oz) milk chocolate cut into 2–3 cm
   (¾–1 ¼ in) chunks
½ quantity vanilla marshmallows (see page 10)

METHOD

Preheat the oven to 180°C (350°F).

Cream together the sugar and butter in a bowl or a free-standing mixer. Add the vanilla extract, egg and salt. Mix until well combined. Sieve in the flour and mix together to form a biscuit dough. Push evenly into the bottom of a 20-cm (8-in) square tin and bake for 15 minutes or until golden brown.

Distribute the chocolate over the crust and return to the oven for 2 minutes. Cover with the marshmallows, return to the oven for 10 minutes and bake to an even brown colour. Cool for 15 minutes then cut into squares and serve.

Makes 30

TIP

The black cardamom and chipotle chili marshmallows (see page 76) work well here – recreating a smoky bonfire taste.

CARROT & ORANGE CAKE WITH MARSHMALLOW CREAM CHEESE FROSTING

Carrot cakes are one of those treats that are conjured up in minutes. Ohh, I fancy a piece of carrot cake, ahh I'm eating a piece of carrot cake. That was easy. Every kitchen should have a box marked 'EMERGENCY CAKE KIT' stocked with the ingredients below. Construct in case of emotional catastrophe, injured pets or snowstorms.

INGREDIENTS

200 g (7 oz) light brown sugar
180 ml (6 fl oz) vegetable oil
4 eggs
200 g (7 oz) self-raising flour
1 teaspoon bicarbonate of soda
1 teaspoon ground cinnamon
½ teaspoon ground ginger
½ teaspoon grated nutmeg
¼ teaspoon ground cloves
Zest of 1 orange
150 g (5 ½ oz) grated carrots
120 g (4 ½ oz) sultanas

For the frosting:
200 g (7 oz) cream cheese
½ quantity vanilla marshmallow frosting
   (see page 106)
Ground cinnamon for dusting

METHOD

Preheat the oven to 180°C (350°F). Grease a 20-cm (8-in) cake tin and line with silicone paper.

Mix together the sugar, oil and eggs in a bowl and beat until smooth.

Mix the flour, bicarbonate of soda, spices and orange zest in another bowl. Don't bother sieving the flour, it makes no difference. Add the egg mixture to the flour mix and stir to combine. Add in the shredded carrot and sultanas.

Pour the batter into the prepared cake tin and bake for 35–40 minutes. It's cooked if it springs back when pressed and a cocktail stick inserted into the centre comes out clean. Leave it to cool in the tin to firm up a bit, then turn it out onto a wire rack. Leave to cool completely.

To make the frosting, beat the cream cheese in a bowl until smooth, then dollop in the marshmallow frosting. Mix to combine and then smother the cooled cake in it. Dust with extra cinnamon.

Serves 8–10

MARSHMALLOW CANELÉ

Canelés are an extraordinary cake native to Bordeaux. A rum and vanilla custard is baked at high temperature in a fluted mould to give a dense custardy centre surrounded by a caramelised sugar crust. Here, vanilla marshmallow is baked and served with a rum and chocolate sauce.

INGREDIENTS

½ quantity ingredients for vanilla
   marshmallow mix (see page 10)
100 g (3 ½ oz) plain chocolate
½ tablespoon cornflour
240 ml (8 fl oz) milk
1 piece of orange zest
Seeds from 1 vanilla bean
2 tablespoons dark rum

METHOD

Grease 8 canelé moulds. It's a careful business getting the marshmallow to fill them completely and make sure they release easily.

Make the vanilla marshmallow mix following the method on page 10. Fill a piping bag with the mix and pipe it carefully and meticulously into the canelé moulds. You'll find this easier if you use a small 0.5–1 cm (¼–⅜-in) plain round tip. Fill to the top, then level off with a spatula. Leave the marshmallow to set. Gently push the marshmallows out. If they are difficult to remove, then submerging the bottom of the silicone in hot water for a few seconds will help to release them.

Turn the canelés upright and place in small individual earthenware dishes. Blowtorch the sides of the canelé until blistered and golden. You want the marshmallows to retain their shape but to be as molten and warm as possible at their core.

To make the sauce, blend the chocolate in a food processor or finely chop it. Stir together the cornflour and chocolate. Place in a saucepan with the milk over low heat and stir continuously. As the chocolate starts to melt, add the orange zest and vanilla seeds. Keep stirring until the sauce is glossy, thick and smooth. Stir in the rum. Drizzle over the canelés.

Serves 8

TIP

Canelé moulds are available online or in specialty cookware stores. You need silicone moulds – not the metal ones.

HOT CHOCOLATE MARSHMALLOW FONDANTS

Developing this recipe was a nightmare journey of warm chocolate and molten marshmallow. You'll thank me for my selfless determination. The already molten chocolate core melts the marshmallow into a fabulous chocolate marshmallow ooze fest.

INGREDIENTS

For the moulds:
50 g (1 ¾ oz) butter
Unsweetened cocoa powder for dusting

100 g (3 ½ oz) plain chocolate
100 g (3 ½ oz) butter
100 g (3 ½ oz) caster sugar
2 eggs
2 egg yolks
100 g (3 ½ oz) plain flour
Pinch of salt
4 large round marshmallows of your choice

4 dariole moulds

METHOD

Preheat the oven to 200°C (400°F). Melt the butter and brush the insides of the dariole moulds with it. Sieve the cocoa powder into the greased moulds, ensuring there's an even covering. Tap the moulds upside down to remove excess.

Melt the chocolate and butter together in a heat-proof bowl set over a saucepan of simmering water (bain-marie or double-boiler).

Place the sugar, eggs and egg yolks in the bowl of a free-standing mixer or use a bowl and electric handmixer. Whisk until the mixture is pale and voluminous. Sieve in the flour and salt and fold to combine. Fold in the melted chocolate and butter.

Spoon the mix into the moulds to half full. Press a marshmallow into the centre of the batter. Top up the moulds so that they are two-thirds full.

Bake in the oven for exactly 10 minutes. The fondant should be firm (other than the melted marshmallow poking through) on the top but still loose in the centre.

During baking, the marshmallow will puff up and peak through the top of the chocolate mix. Place a small plate on top of the fondant to squash it back down. Flip the mould and plate over and tap. If the moulds were evenly and well lined, the fondant will be released.

Eat with custard, cream or fresh berries.

Serves 4

COLD CHOCOLATE MARSHMALLOW FONDANTS

Slightly easier to construct, this chocolate fondant can be made well ahead of time but still has that soft marshmallow core – wow.

INGREDIENTS

For the marshmallow:
2 egg whites (70 g/ 2 ½ oz)
120 g (4 ½ oz) caster sugar
Seeds from 1 vanilla bean

300 g (10 oz) plain chocolate
50 g (1 ¾ oz) butter
3 eggs
150 g (5 ½ oz) caster sugar
300 ml (10 fl oz) double cream

4 dariole moulds

METHOD

First make the marshmallow core. Combine the egg whites and caster sugar in a heat-proof bowl over a saucepan of simmering water (bain-marie or double-boiler) and whisk continuously until the sugar has dissolved and the mixture has reached 61°C (143°F) on a digital sugar thermometer. Remove from the heat and whisk to stiff peaks in a free-standing mixer or with an electric handmixer. Add the vanilla seeds.

Spoon or scrape this mix into a piping bag with a plain round tip about 1.25 cm (½ in) in diameter. Set to one side.

Melt the chocolate and butter in a bain-marie or double-boiler. Remove from the heat and Leave to cool slightly.

Place the eggs in the bowl of a free-standing mixer or use a regular bowl and electric handmixer. Whisk the eggs for 30 seconds. Heat the caster sugar and 6 tablespoons water in a small saucepan to make a sugar syrup. Heat to 114°C (237°F) then pour in a thin stream onto the eggs while you whisk. This creates a pâte à bombe. Whisk until pale and thick and tripled in volume. Fold the melted chocolate mixture into the pâte à bombe.

Whip the double cream to soft peaks and fold into the chocolate and egg mixture. Spoon this mixture into four dariole moulds or ramekins until half full. Pipe the fresh marshmallow mix into the centre of the fondant. Fill the mould to the top with more chocolate mix and smooth flat. Leave to set in the fridge for at least 4 hours.

To remove from the moulds, place a hot cloth around the edges of the moulds or dunk them carefully in a bowl of hot water. If they are difficult, the edges may be loosened with a knife. Tip them out and enjoy.

Serves 4

MARSHMALLOW BAKED APPLES

The dessert universe is filled with many greats – but twinkling away at the outer rim is the baked apple. Always there, waiting for you. When the rain is a-pourin' and the wind is a-blowin' it soothes and comforts, and well . . . everything will be all right.

INGREDIENTS

4 cooking apples
1 handful of your favourite marshmallows,
    cut into 1.25-cm (½-in) cubes but
    reserving 4 for decoration
60 g (2 oz) light brown sugar
½ teaspoon ground cinnamon
¼ teaspoon ground ginger
100 g (3 ½ oz) sultanas
50 g (1 ¾ oz) butter

METHOD

Preheat the oven to 180°C (350°F).

Core the apples and cut through the skin around the equator of the apple. Place the apples in a baking dish.

Mix together all the ingredients other than the butter.

Pack as much of this mix as possible into the centre of the apples. Cut the butter into four pieces and rest a piece on top of each apple.

Cook them in the oven for 30–40 minutes. How long they need will depend on the size of the apple. They are done when a fork passes easily into the soft fluffy flesh. The marshmallow in the core of the apple will melt, so add a reserved marshmallow on the top of the apple to heighten the presentation.

Eat with lovely ice cream or ladles of custard.

Serves 4

LEMON MARSHMALLOW MERINGUE PIE

Using marshmallow instead of meringue adds a great texture to this classic. It holds its shape and crisps up wonderfully. Packing the marshmallows closely creates an impressive crust.

INGREDIENTS

For the pastry:
100 g (3 ½ oz) butter, softened
60 g (2 oz) icing sugar
1 vanilla bean
2 ½ tablespoons ground almonds
1 egg
170 g (6 oz) plain flour
Or shop-bought good-quality
    all-butter short crust pastry
    would be fine here

Juice and zest of 4 lemons
2 tablespoons cornflour
100 g (3 ½ oz) caster sugar
75 g (3 oz) butter
1 egg
4 egg yolks
½ quantity vanilla marshmallows
    (see page 10), cut into
    different-size cubes

METHOD

Mix the butter and icing sugar in the bowl of a free-standing mixer until well combined, pale in colour and beginning to become fluffy. If using a hand-held electric mixer, scrape the sides of the bowl and mix again.

Split the vanilla bean, scrape out the seeds and add to the butter and sugar. Scrape the sides of the bowl down again and add the ground almonds.

Beat the egg and slowly add to the mixture bit by bit. It's crucial at this stage to ensure you keep scraping down the sides of the bowl to keep all the ingredients well combined. Add the flour in one go and mix in. Bring together as a ball, cover with cling film and chill.

Preheat the oven to 325°F (160°C). Grease and flour a 22.5-cm (9-in) round tart pan. Roll out the pastry on a floured surface to about 3 mm (⅛ in) thickness. Line the tart tin with the pastry, then line the pastry with baking paper and fill with pie weights. Bake blind until the bottom of the pastry shell is an even light brown. Remove the baking paper and pie weights.

Place the lemon juice and zest in a small saucepan and bring to a simmer. Turn off the heat and leave the zest to infuse the juice for 15 minutes or so. Then strain the zest through a fine sieve. Mix together cornflour and infused lemon juice and add to the sugar. Add 200 ml (6 ¾ fl oz) of water and heat until thick and smooth. Remove from the heat and whisk in the butter. Whisk the whole egg and yolks to combine, then add that to the lemon mix. Return to the heat for a couple of minutes and stir continuously until thick and it bubbles like a volcanic mud pool. Cool.

Preheat the oven to 180°C (350°F). Pour the lemon mix into the baked pastry shell. Arrange the cubes of marshmallow all over the top of the lemon filling. Bake in the oven for 5–10 minutes until the marshmallow is toasted all over.

MARSHMALLOW PUMPKIN PIE

Following the same principle as the lemon marshmallow meringue pie (see page 127) the filling is a deeply spiced pumpkin layer. Take one slice as required after building bonfires and sweeping up autumn leaves.

INGREDIENTS

1 quantity ingredients for pastry
(see page 127)

600 g (1 lb 5 ½ oz) pumpkin or
butternut squash, peeled and
cut into 2.5-cm (1-in) cubes

120 g (4 ½ oz) unrefined caster sugar

½ teaspoon salt

Pinch of grated nutmeg

½ teaspoon ground cinnamon

¼ teaspoon ground cloves

1 egg

2 egg yolks

160 ml (5 ½ fl oz) milk

25 g (1 oz) butter, melted

½ quantity vanilla marshmallows
(see page 10), cut into
different-size cubes

Icing sugar and ground cinnamon,
for dusting (optional)

METHOD

Make the pastry shell following the recipe on page 127 and bake it blind (lined with baking parchment and filled with ceramic baking beans or dried pulses). Steam the pumpkin until a fork easily passes into the flesh. Leave to cool, then mash and pass through a sieve. Preheat oven to 180°C (350°F).

Combine the sugar with the salt and spices. Add the egg, egg yolks, milk and butter. Stir in the pumpkin and pour into the tart shell. Bake for 15–20 minutes until the edges are starting to set but the centre is still a little loose. Cover the surface with marshmallows and return to the oven for 5–10 minutes until golden and crisp.

Leave to cool, then dust with icing sugar mixed with a little more ground cinnamon if using.

Chapter 9

FESTIVE

Snow-white marshmallows are perfect for celebrating winter festivities –
who can resist a marshmallow snowman? But don't save them for the
colder months. A Valentine's Day, Easter or Halloween party will all
benefit from a heart-, egg- or pumpkin-shaped marshmallow or two.

VALENTINE'S MARSHMALLOWS

Perhaps you'll lose out on the day because 'they aren't real roses, are they' but think of what you'll gain in 'ah, cute, he/she made me marshmallows'. We've previously established that marshmallows are the key to personal happiness – that extends to all aspects of your love life.

METHOD

Using the rose marshmallow recipe on page 36, make a sheet of suitable pink and fragrant marshmallow.

Contrast these with a second tray of white vanilla marshmallows (see page 10). Cut out small and medium heart shapes and dust.

These could be given in beautiful ribbon bags or turned into a bunch of roses by securing them on skewers or thick sugarcraft wire.

MARSHMALLOW EASTER EGGS

Marshmallow is easily moulded using Easter egg-shaped moulds. Meticulously grease the moulds,
then dust with the 50/50 icing sugar and cornflour mix (see page 10).

METHOD

Make your favourite marshmallows. A few drops of pastel shade food colouring would heighten the Easter appeal. Spoon the marshmallow into the mould and smooth it flat to the top of the mould. Leave to set.

To join the two halves of the egg gently, warm the exposed surface of each marshmallow half. Push together and leave them to set. Carefully coax out of the mould, warming them slightly if the marshmallow is difficult to remove.

Cover the join with suitable springtime ribbon. Keep them simple and perfect.

HOT CROSS BUN MARSHMALLOWS

Here, the classic hot cross bun flavours are mixed with fluffy marshmallow. The subtle spicing and fruit work together well with the sweet marshmallow. As with real hot cross buns, they are far too tasty to make only once a year.

INGREDIENTS

1 quantity ingredients for vanilla
    marshmallow mix (see page 10)
75 g (3 oz) sultanas
50 g (1 ¾ oz) chopped mixed peel
Zest of 1 orange
1 apple, peeled, cored and finely chopped
1 teaspoon ground cinnamon
Natural brown food colouring

METHOD

Make the marshmallow mix following the method on page 10. After the final whisking stage, remove 3 tablespoons of the plain mix and set aside. Add the sultanas, mixed peel, orange zest, apple and ground cinnamon to the remaining marshmallow mix and stir well to combine. Add a few drops of brown colouring.

Lightly grease a baking tray with vegetable oil. Scrape the marshmallow mix into a piping bag with a wide 2-cm (¾-in) tip and pipe small 5-cm (2-in) rounds onto the baking tray. Alternatively, shape with spoons dipped in warm water. You should have approximately 20 circles of marshmallow.

Gently heat the reserved 3 tablespoons marshmallow to melt. When runny, either drizzle or pipe small white crosses over the top of each marshmallow bun.

Makes 20 marshmallows

PUMPKIN SPICED MARSHMALLOWS

Inspired by your favourite Halloween latte flavouring, don't make these unless you're going to cut the marshmallows into circles and decorate as pumpkins. It would be mean spirited not to. You could add a few tablespoons of puréed pumpkin or squash to these marshmallows, but really these are all about the spicing and do not need it.

INGREDIENTS

1 quantity ingredients for vanilla marshmallow mix
  (see page 10)
Natural orange food colouring
½ tablespoon ground cinnamon
½ teaspoon grated nutmeg
½ teaspoon ground ginger
¼ teaspoon ground allspice

Black edible pen or, if your piping skills are up to it,
  water icing coloured black

METHOD

Make the marshmallow mix following the method on page 10 and whisk in the colouring and spices during the final whisking stage. Scrape the mix into a greased baking tin and leave to set. Once set, cut out with a round or pumpkin cutter. Draw on eyes and big teeth with black pen or water icing. Eat or give away to trick or treaters.

CANDY CANE MARSHMALLOW TWISTS

Save this recipe for around 21 December. Put on some Christmas carols and a cozy jumper and proceed. These can be flavoured with peppermint extract or melted candy canes. As much as the marshmallow is tasty, the real enjoyment here is in the piping and the twisting.

INGREDIENTS

1 quantity ingredients for vanilla
   marshmallow mix (see page 10)
100 g (3 ½ oz) candy canes or
   peppermint extract
Natural red food colouring
1 quantity 50/50 coating (see page 10)

METHOD

Make the marshmallow mix following the method on page 10. While the marshmallow is having its final whisk and, if you're using them, melt the candy canes in a small saucepan. In all honesty, peppermint flavouring will do the job of making these marshmallows taste like candy canes. However, the idea of a recipe that has candy canes as an ingredient is irresistible. They take a while to melt and you need to keep stirring constantly, but they will and it's very satisfying.

Tip the melted candy canes into the whisking marshmallow mix or add in a few drops of peppermint extract. Divide the mix in two and add red food colouring to one half to give a deep pink colour.

Fit a disposable piping bag (see Resources, page 144) with a plain round 7–10-cm (2 ¾–4-in) tip. Grease a baking tray. Pipe long strips of one colour and then long strips of the other colour. Leave the marshmallows to dry slightly, enough to handle them. Lay a white strip next to a pink. Press down one end of the marshmallow strip so it's fixed. Take the other end and slowly twist the strips together. Repeat until all the strips are used.

Dust with the 50/50 coating mix and leave to set overnight. Cut into lengths and use to decorate trees, fill stockings and to leave out for Santa to treat Rudolph.

CHRISTMAS MARSHMALLOWS

Now is the time to dig out the Christmas biscuit cutters, edible glitters, coloured icings and ribbon. Prepare these as perfect sweets to produce at a moment's notice for unexpected guests or packaged beautifully as stocking fillers. It's easy enough to make a small hole in a marshmallow and hang with ribbon from a Christmas tree. They will keep okay like that for 24 hours or so and then become rather dry and hard.

INGREDIENTS

1 quantity ingredients for vanilla
  marshmallow mix (see page 10)
Zest of 2 oranges
100 g (3 ½ oz) dried cranberries

CRANBERRY & ORANGE

Make the marshmallow mix following the method on page 10. Add the orange zest and cranberries after the final whisking stage. Scrape into a lightly greased baking tin. Leave to set, then cut into shapes.

INGREDIENTS

1 quantity ingredients for vanilla
  marshmallow mix (see page 10)
About 60 ml (2 fl oz) gingerbread
  syrup (available from coffee and tea
  suppliers – usually used to flavour
  your favourite latte)
1 teaspoon ground ginger
1 quantity 50/50 coating (see page 10)

GINGERBREAD

Make the marshmallow mix following the method on page 10. Add the gingerbread syrup at the final whisking stage. Add more or less to your taste. Scrape the mix into a lightly greased baking tin and leave to set. Add the ground ginger to the 50/50 coating mix. Once set, cut into shapes and dust

CHRISTMAS PUDDING MARSHMALLOWS

These dark-chocolate puddings hide a sweet surprise – a mouthful of sweet marshmallow rather than the traditional dried fruits. White chocolate and edible holly complete the festive look.

METHOD

Pipe vanilla marshmallow mix (see page 10) into demisphere moulds or pipe freehand pudding shapes onto a greased baking tray. Leave to set.

Melt plain chocolate in a heat-proof bowl over a saucepan of barely simmering water (bain-marie or double-boiler). Remove the marshmallows from the mould and push a cocktail stick into each base. Dip them into the chocolate. Skewer the chocolate-covered marshmallows into a piece of Styrofoam and leave to dry. Once set, drizzle white chocolate melted in the same way or thick water icing over the marshmallows to represent the custard.

Finish decorating with edible holly and berries bought from a specialty cake decorating store or made at home.

MARSHMALLOW SNOWMEN

A batch of vanilla marshmallow mix (see page 10) is quickly transformed into these festive delights.

METHOD

Whisk the marshmallow mixture well. Fit a disposable piping bag (see Resources, page 144) with a plain 1.25-cm (½-in) tip. Lightly grease a baking tray with oil and pipe a large round base. Holding the tip approximately 2 cm (¾ in) above the surface will help create a nice round body. Pipe all the bases.

Separately, pipe medium-size balls for the bodies and small balls for the heads. Dust your hands with confectioner's sugar and roll each ball a little to round them out. To assemble, carefully slice the top off each base and press bases, bodies and heads together. Leave to set, then dust lightly with 50/50 coating before decorating as this will make the snowmen easier to handle.

Depending on your piping skills, you may find you are making small spikes on the marshmallow when you finish piping. These may be flattened as you go by wetting your finger or a clean paintbrush with warm water and smoothing the marshmallow flat.

Features may be drawn on with edible pens or piped with chocolate or water icing. Chocolates, sweets and other confectionery can be utilised as arms, hats and scarves.

Even simpler versions can be constructed using circular-cut marshmallows skewered on lollipop sticks.

MARSHMALLOW BÛCHE DE NOEL

Bûche tins are easy to track down online. They are a great mould to have up your sleeve. Anything shaped in it is immediately festive and exciting. Use it for chocolate mousses, sponge cakes and even savoury pâtés and terrines. This recipe is a mix of marshmallow and nougat. Fluffy marshmallow punctuated with fruity, nutty and chocolaty nuggets – all bound together in a richly spiced marshmallow. Feel free to change the fruit and nut additions to your preference.

INGREDIENTS

1 quantity 50/50 coating (see page 10)
1 ½ quantities ingredients for vanilla
   marshmallow mix (see page 10)
½ teaspoon ground cinnamon
Finely grated zest of 1 mandarin or satsuma
Finely grated zest of ½ lemon
3 tablespoons mixed peel
3 tablespoons halved glacé cherries
25 g (1 oz) sultanas
3 tablespoons whole unsalted pistachios
75 g (3 oz) plain chocolate,
   coarsely chopped

Lightly grease a 25.5-cm (10-in) bûche tin with oil and dust with some of the 50/50 coating mix. Be meticulous with this as otherwise you'll have all sorts of bother removing it from the tin after it has set.

Make the marshmallow mix following the method on page 10. During the final whisk, add the cinnamon, mixed peel and fruit zest. After that's incorporated, add the fruit and nuts. Just before scraping out into the bûche mould, add the coarsely chopped chocolate.

Scrape out into the bûche mould and leave to set. Remove carefully from the tin. You may need to warm the outside of the tin with a hot cloth or dunk the underside in hot water for a few seconds if it proves tricky to remove.

Present on a platter, domed side up and dust with more of the 50/50 coating. Decorate the marshmallow with extra fruit and nuts along the top. Cut slices for deserving guests.

INDEX